the world series

MARK STEWART

FRANKLIN WATTS

A Division of Scholastic Inc.

New York • Toronto • London • Auckland • Sydney

Mexico City • New Delhi • Hong Kong

Danbury, Connecticut

Cover design by Dave Klaboe   Series design by Molly Heron

Cover photo IDs: (center) Tommy Herr makes a double play; (clockwise from upper left) Jackie Robinson, Bernie Williams at the 2000 World Series, Franklin D. Roosevelt throwing the first pitch in 1932, Cleveland Indians pitcher Dennis Martinez in 1999, opening ceremonies at the 2001 World Series, Babe Ruth with his daughter Dorothy in 1928.

Photographs © 2002: AP/Wide World Photos: 115 (Harry Cabluck), 146 (Eric Draper), cover right center (Mark Duncan), 145 (Ron Frehm), 133 (Rusty Kennedy), 138 (Jim Mone), cover top center (Amy Sancetta), 127 (Cliff Schiappa), cover bottom left, 49, 50, 57, 79, 82, 101, 103, 104, 116, 117, 120; Corbis Images: cover bottom, 148 (AFP), cover top left, cover center, cover top right, 20, 33, 36, 39, 42, 46, 53, 59, 62, 64, 66, 73, 74, 75, 80, 83, 84, 89, 91, 93, 98, 99, 108, 110, 122, 124, 128 (Bettman), 85 (Sonnee Gottlieb/Bettman), 137 (Martin Jeong/Bettman), 27 (Kit Kittle), 134 (George Nikitin/Bettman), 150, 151 (Reuters NewMedia Inc.); National Baseball Hall of Fame Library, Cooperstown, N.Y.: 88 (AP Photo), 76 (Corbis), 4, 7, 16, 21, 22, 31, 54; Photodisc, Inc./C Squared Studios: 160; Team Stewart, Inc.: 78 (Ebony/Johnson Publishing), 11 (Goodwin & Co., 1888), 13, 14 (Harper's Weekly, 1888), 26 (H.M. Fechheimer), 29 (P.F. Collier & Son), 142 (Sport Illustrated/Time Inc.), 95 (Street & Smith Publications, Inc.), 28 (Tom Barker Co., 1913), 106 (Topps Chewing Gum, Inc.), 45 (Underwood & Underwood), 143 (USA Today Baseball Weekly).

Library of Congress Cataloging-in-Publication Data

Stewart, Mark.
    The World Series / Mark Stewart.
    p. cm. — (The Watts history of sports)
    Includes bibliographical references and index.
    Summary: A year-by-year account of the World Series games from
    the 1800s through the twenty-first century.
    ISBN 0-531-11953-X (lib. bdg.)
    1. World Series (Baseball)—History—Juvenile literature. [1. World Series (Baseball)—
    History. 2. Baseball—History.] 1. Title. II. Series.
    GV878.4 .S76 2002
    796.357'646'09—dc21   2001005727

CONTENTS

Avenue Grounds in Cincinnati was typical of most major-league parks during the early days of professional baseball. The wooden grandstand held only a couple thousand spectators. For big games, fans were allowed to overflow on to the field.

INTRODUCTION

In the years before the Civil War (1861–65), baseball was played primarily in the major northeastern cities of the United States. Playing customs differed slightly from city to city and, in some cases, from neighborhood to neighborhood. Until the mid-1850s, some of baseball's most basic rules were not firmly established. The concept of a World Series simply did not exist.

In the Civil War, people who had never experienced much of anything went through an experience that would change their lives. The young men who survived the long, bloody conflict came home with a new attitude toward winning and losing. Victory brought glory; defeat brought humiliation. Winning was suddenly important. To some, it meant everything.

This had not always been the case. In the first half of the 19th century, winning was not an important part of sports. The primary goal of sports was exercise. Any type of athletics that caused a participant to injure himself—or even to sweat—was regarded as foolish.

Many Civil War soldiers had played baseball before. But with all those young people coming together from so many parts of the country, a newer, more competitive version of baseball emerged. This was the game that the soldiers brought home with them, and it was played much better—and much harder—than ever before. It was played to win.

In no time, baseball became America's national obsession. Those who could play it did, and those who could not started paying

to watch it. By the end of the 1860s, hundreds of players were being compensated for their skills. The first all-professional team was formed in 1869. Within two years, there were enough pro teams to form a professional league: the National Association.

The National Association played from 1871 to 1875. In 1876, the National League (NL) was formed. In the early years, NL teams played two or three official games a week, plus unofficial exhibitions against other NL clubs and some semiprofessional

---

STATISTICS KEY

2B = Double
3B = Triple
BA = Batting Average
CG = Complete Game
GS = Game(s) Started
ER = Earned Run(s)
ERA = Earned Run Average
GW RBI = Game-Winning RBI
H = Hit(s)
HR = Home Run(s)
IP = Inning(s) Pitched
K = Strikeout(s)
OBA = On-Base Average
R = Run(s)
RBI = Run Batted In
SA = Slugging Average
SB = Stolen Base(s)
SV = Save(s)
W = Win(s)
XBH = Extra-Base Hit(s)

squads. At the end of the season, the team with the most league victories was declared the "pennant" winner. The National League continues to operate today.

Professional baseball struggled during its first few years. On average, only 250,000 fans per season paid to watch league games. Almost every year, one or two clubs went out of business. Sometimes they were replaced with new franchises, but sometimes they were not.

By the 1880s, baseball had become popular enough as a spectator sport for the formation of a second league. The American Association (AA) began play in 1882. Knowing that many working-class fans wanted to watch baseball but could not afford tickets, the association decided to charge $.25 admission—half the NL's cheapest ticket. It also decided to relax rules about alcohol consumption in its ball parks and embraced attendance-building promotions such as Ladies Day. At first, National League owners thought their AA rivals would go bankrupt, but the AA's business practices proved to be quite profitable. It was clear that this league would not go away.

At the end of the 1882 season, the Chicago White Stockings stood atop the NL standings. The Cincinnati Reds—who had been thrown out of the NL for selling beer in the stands—took the AA pennant. Chicago agreed to play an exhibition series against the second-place Providence Grays, but on their way east, they stopped in Cincinnati to play an exhibition series with the Reds. This marked the very first time two baseball pennant winners played each other.

History has a funny way of rewriting itself. As mentioned, postseason (and even in-season) exhibition games were commonplace in baseball, so there was little mention in the sporting press of these games being baseball's first true "championship" series. Over time, however, this innocent meeting has taken on a life of its own. To those seeking the true roots of the World Series, the 1882 exhibition matches have become a popular starting point.

THE 19th CENTURY

1882
Chicago White Stockings (NL) vs. Cincinnati Reds (AA)

The Chicago White Stockings put together a marvelous stretch run in 1882, winning 16 of their last 17 contests to capture the National League pennant by three games over the Providence Grays. The team's top hitters were infielders King Kelly, Ned Williamson, and Cap Anson. Anson was Chicago's player-manager and the game's greatest star. Leading the White Stockings' mound crew were Larry Corcoran and Fred Goldsmith. Corcoran let his catcher know what type of pitch he planned to throw by shifting his tobacco chaw to different locations in his mouth, while Goldsmith was an expert with the magical and mysterious curveball.

The Reds ran away with the American Association flag. Two key holdovers from the old NL club—pitcher Will White and third baseman Hick Carpenter—did the bulk of the work for the Reds, along with veteran catcher (and manager) Pop Snyder and young Bid McPhee, a defensive whiz at second base. Chicago, coming off its third straight pennant, was a huge favorite.

By the sixth inning of the first game, the

Adrian "Cap" Anson, the top player and manager in baseball during the 1880s. His White Stockings participated in the first championship series.

fans at Cincinnati's Bank Street Grounds realized they were witnessing a bit of baseball history. Their Reds were playing every bit as well as the great White Stockings. With the score tied 0-0 going into the bottom of the seventh inning, Carpenter stroked a one-out single off Goldsmith and then advanced to third on a single by Dan Stearns. Chick Fulmer followed with a single to center for the game's first run. McPhee, a small man with good power, cracked a triple to right center-field to make the score 3-0. He later came home on a wild pitch. The game ended 4-0 on a spectacular play at the plate. White allowed just eight hits in shutting out Chicago.

A capacity crowd showed up the next day to watch White work again, this time against Corcoran. A pair of first-inning errors set up two Chicago runs, which scored thanks to a new bit of strategy: the hit-and-run. Used extensively by Boston and Baltimore a decade later, this play was actually unveiled by Anson during this first World Series. White allowed just three more hits after the first inning, but the Reds could not solve Corcoran, and the game ended 2-0. Unfortunately, this was the last game played. American Association president Denny McKnight, who believed the NL was bent on ruining the AA, threatened to throw the Reds out if they continued to play the NL champs. There would be no fraternizing with the enemy.

Reds 1
  Best Player: Doc White
                (18 IP, 0.00 ERA)

White Stockings 1
  Best Player: Ned Williamson
                (.500 BA)

This situation was resolved a couple of months later, when the NL and the AA signed a peace agreement. This pact did not include plans for any postseason championship games, and none were played in 1883. The AA champion Philadelphia Athletics did challenge the NL champion Boston Beaneaters to a series in late October. But during an exhibition tour after the season, the Athletics lost seven of eight games. Philadelphia manager Lew Simmons decided to cancel the meetings with Boston because he feared that no one would show up to watch them.

The 1882 meeting between the Reds and White Stockings is generally regarded as a typical exhibition meeting. Neither team was aware that it was playing for a championship. Beginning with the 1884 series between Providence and New York, however, it is fair to say that fans and players alike knew that a championship was on the line.

1884
Providence Grays (NL) vs. New York Metropolitans (AA)

The Grays took the National League pennant on the strong right arm of Old Hoss Radbourn, who became the only pitcher to win 60 games in a season. Around midseason, with the Grays in a tight race and number-two starter Charlie Sweeney causing problems, Radbourn (then 24-8) made a deal to pitch all of Providence's remaining games in exchange for the club's promise to free him from his contract after the season.

In the American Association, the Mets emerged from an exciting five-team race thanks to their twin 37-game winners,

Tim Keefe and Jack Lynch, as well as the remarkable hitting of Dave Orr, who batted .354 and collected more than 300 total bases.

New York manager Jim Mutrie issued a postseason challenge to the Grays to play a three-game exhibition, with each team putting up $1,000. The Grays would have to play by AA rules, which still did not permit pitchers to throw overhand. Radbourn, a side-armer, was not affected by this agreement, and he dominated the Mets in Game One. Keefe kept pace and allowed just one hit going into the seventh inning. But the Grays bunched four hard hits and went on to win 6-0 behind Radbourn's two-hitter.

The two pitching stars faced each other the next day, and again the Grays struck first. They took a 3-0 lead on a home run over the leftfield fence by slugger Jerry Denny. The Mets scored once in the bottom of the fifth, on an infield single and two errors. The game was called in the eighth inning when it became too dark to play, and Providence was awarded the 3-1 victory.

With the series already "decided," the weather turning nasty, and only 500 paying customers in the park, the Grays asked if they could skip the third and final game and go back to Providence. The Mets persuaded the Grays to stay by letting them pick the game's umpire. Manager Frank Bancroft craftily chose New York's own Tim Keefe. This meant that Keefe could not pitch against them! Buck Becannon, a rookie, started for the Mets instead and was battered for 11 runs in 6 innings. Radbourn gave up six hits and two unearned runs for his third great performance of the series.

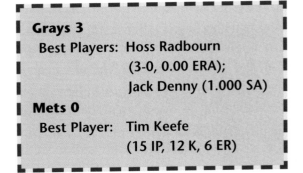

Grays 3
Best Players: Hoss Radbourn (3-0, 0.00 ERA); Jack Denny (1.000 SA)
Mets 0
Best Player: Tim Keefe (15 IP, 12 K, 6 ER)

1885
Chicago White Stockings (NL) vs. St. Louis Browns (AA)

The St. Louis Browns were perfectly built for the 1880s. Led by player-manager Charlie Comiskey, the Browns boasted some of the smartest and most aggressive players in baseball, including Kid Gleason, Curt Welch, and Arlie Latham. They knew how to create runs, and also how to prevent them. Bob Caruthers, just 21 years old, led the club with 40 wins and a 2.07 ERA, while Dave Foutz added 33 victories to help St. Louis win the pennant by a whopping 16 games.

In the National League, the Chicago White Stockings went down to the wire with the New York Giants. Led by the power-hitting quartet of King Kelly, Ned Williamson, Cap Anson, and Abner Dalrymple—as well as pitchers John Clarkson and Jim McCormick—Chicago beat New York three of four games down the stretch to secure the pennant.

The best-of-seven series was scheduled to hit four baseball-hungry Midwestern cities, beginning in Chicago, where the teams played to a 5-5 tie. Game Two, which was held in St. Louis, ended after Anson and Kelly intimidated the umpire into reversing a crucial call. St. Louis fans angrily stormed the field, and the White Stockings, wielding bats in self-defense, fled the scene. Eventually a forfeit was declared, and Chicago got the win. The Browns evened the series with a 7-4 victory, then won again the next day when a local baseball fan named William Medart was pressed into service as umpire. Every close call went St. Louis's way, and the game's final out was recorded when Comiskey playfully tagged a Chicago runner whose foot was planted firmly on first base. Medart claimed that the runner had wandered off the bag, and he called him out. The game went to St. Louis by a score of 3-2.

The two teams traveled to the city of Pittsburgh to play Game Five. Foutz allowed four first-inning runs, and the White Stockings coasted to a 9-2 win. The series moved to Cincinnati for Game Six, where Chicago won an error-plagued contest, again by a score of 9-2. Anson and Comiskey met prior to Game Seven and agreed that the winner would be crowned world champion. Although a St. Louis victory would leave the teams tied 3-3-1, Anson was so certain of his team's chances that he announced grandly that Chicago would not accept the forfeit win from Game Two. Imagine his surprise when Clarkson was late to the ballpark and Anson was forced to send McCormick to the mound for the third day in a row. Jumping all over the exhausted right-hander in the fourth and fifth innings, the Browns scored ten runs and won 13-4 to claim the championship. After the series, team owners Al Spalding and Chris Von der Ahe publicly stated that the series had been a tie. This cheated the St. Louis players of their promised "winner's share" and saved the two men $500 each.

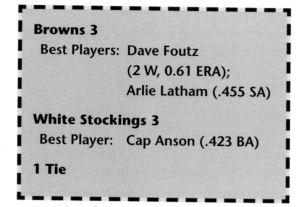

> **Browns 3**
> Best Players: Dave Foutz
>   (2 W, 0.61 ERA);
>   Arlie Latham (.455 SA)
>
> **White Stockings 3**
> Best Player: Cap Anson (.423 BA)
>
> **1 Tie**

1886
Chicago White Stockings (NL) vs. St. Louis Browns (AA)

The cast of characters for this best-of-seven series was nearly identical to the one that assumed center stage the previous fall. The White Stockings were powered by Cap Anson and King Kelly, with John Clarkson winning 36 games and Jim McCormick tallying 31. The Browns were paced once again by hitters Curt Welch, Tip O'Neill, and Arlie Latham, with Dave Foutz and Bob Caruthers teaming up for 71 wins. From a historical standpoint, the most important difference between this meeting and the 1885 championship was that the actual words "World Series" first began to appear. In the Spalding Official Baseball Guide, published in the spring of 1887, the six games played by the Browns and White Stockings were called the World Series.

The opener pitted Foutz against Clarkson. First-inning singles by Anson and second baseman Fred Pfeffer plated a pair of runs against the Browns, and Clarkson went on to win 6-0. In Game Two, the Browns returned the favor with a 12-0 shutout by Caruthers. The offensive spark came from O'Neill, who belted two

Bob Caruthers, a long-forgotten superstar of the 1880s, was the dominant player of the 1886 series.

Game Five was played amidst charges that the Chicagoans were purposely trying to extend the series. Anson refused to put one of his star hurlers on the mound and instead started Williamson, an infielder. The teams had previously agreed that the series would be a winner-take-all affair, with all the gate receipts put into one pot and divided among the winners. The more games played, the bigger the pot. Anson was so confident his team could beat the Browns that he was throwing away Game Five to ensure the series would go the full seven games. The Browns did indeed win, by a 10-3 margin, but Anson's plan blew up in his face the next day. Trailing 3-1 with two on and two out in the eighth inning, the Browns sent Latham to the plate. The brash infielder, known as the "Freshest Man on Earth," turned to the hometown crowd and announced, "Don't get nervous, folks. I'll tie it up." Latham lined a triple to rightfield off Clarkson to knot the score at 3-3. Two innings later, Welch singled for the Browns and advanced to third on an infield single and a bunt. Clarkson, fearing he might steal home, quick-pitched and threw the ball over the catcher's head. Welch arrived home in a cloud of dust with the series-winning run.

inside-the-park home runs. Caruthers talked St. Louis owner Chris Von der Ahe into starting him the next day, but he was hit hard in an 11-4 blowout. The series moved to St. Louis for Game Four. Ten thousand fans showed up at Sportsman's Park to watch the Browns knot the series with an 8-5 victory. A muffed pop-up by Ned Williamson opened the gates to a three-run sixth inning that was the difference for St. Louis.

Browns 4
Best Players: Bob Caruthers
(2 W, 6 R, 5 RBIs);
Tip O'Neill
(.400 BA, 2 HR)

White Stockings 2
Best Player: Fred Pfeffer
(7 R, 4 RBIs)

1887
Detroit Wolverines (NL) vs. St. Louis Browns (AA)

The Browns returned to the top of the American Association with ease, thanks to a Triple Crown season from Tip O'Neill, who batted .435 with 14 home runs and 123 RBIs. Three other Browns—Curt Welch, Charlie Comiskey, and Dave Foutz—knocked in more than 100 runs, while six of the St. Louis regulars scored 100 or more. The pitching staff included Foutz and Bob Caruthers, but the top winner was a teenager named Silver King, who had won one game the year before for the NL's Kansas City Cowboys. King's 32 wins gave the Browns the best three-man rotation in baseball. The Wolverines beat the hard-charging Phillies and the White Stockings (who had sold or traded many of their stars) thanks largely to the timely hitting of Sam Thompson. He knocked in 164 runs—50 percent more than any other batter in the NL that year. Thompson's heavy-hitting teammate, Dan Brouthers, also had a great year. Among the team's other stars were Fred Dunlap, Deacon White, and Ned Hanlon. The pitching staff was solid but unspectacular. Charlie Getzien, a crafty 29-game winner, was the Wolverines' ace.

Because the Wolverines played in the then-small city of Detroit, the best chance owner Frederick Stearns had of playing in front of big crowds and "cashing in" on his champions was to play the championship series as an exhibition tour. Stearns and St. Louis owner Chris Von der Ahe agreed to crisscross the country on a special train. They played 15 games between October 10 and 26—including a game in Washington, D.C., and another in Baltimore on the same

day! Caruthers won the opener, as well as Game Five, but Detroit won every other game through Game Nine. With a 7 games to 2 lead, the Wolverines could have (and probably should have) claimed the world championship, but the tour was due to swing back west anyway, so the two teams kept on playing.

Crowds were decent for the first eight contests, but they quickly dwindled from many thousands to few hundreds. Game Twelve, in Brooklyn, drew just 500 fans; Game Fourteen, in Chicago, was viewed by fewer than 400. The Wolverines won ten games to St. Louis's five. Only four of the games were any good; the rest were one-sided. The top batter for the series was Thompson, who hit .362. O'Neill managed just 13 hits and finished at .200.

> **Wolverines 10**
> Best Players: Charlie Getzien (4 W); Jack Rowe (12 R, 7 RBIs)
> **Browns 5**
> Best Player: Bob Caruthers (4 W, 71 2/3 IP)

1888
New York Giants (NL) vs. St. Louis Browns (AA)

The Browns accomplished one of the great feats in 19th-century baseball by taking their fourth straight pennant in 1888. They finished just ahead of the Brooklyn Bridegrooms, to whom they had traded Bob Caruthers and Dave Foutz over the winter. St. Louis made the trades believing that Silver King would continue to improve, and he did, winning 45 games. The Browns got the usual good season from Arlie Latham, Tip O'Neill, and Charlie Comiskey, as well as Tommy McCarthy, a quick and clever outfielder purchased from the minors. Their opponents in the championship series were the New York Giants.

The Giants had been a fourth-place team in 1887, but they found their stride in 1888, when pitcher Tim Keefe reeled off a 19-game winning streak in the middle of the season. The club also featured Buck Ewing, Roger Connor, and Monte Ward, who were larger than life in both appearance and on-field exploits. Other than these four stars, the Giants were a fairly ordinary club with very good pitching—their ERA was a half-run lower than anyone else's. The format for this October was a best-of-eleven series.

As expected, the highlight of the series was the confrontation between Keefe and King. Keefe outdueled King in Games One, Three, and Five, and the Giants also won Games Four and Six behind Cannonball Crane and Mickey Welch. The turning point in the series was the fifth game, the last scheduled for New York's Polo Grounds. The Browns led 4-1 going into the eighth inning, which, due to darkness, would be the last. Three St. Louis errors and triples by Ewing and Connor produced four runs and a grand comeback victory.

As the series headed to St. Louis with the Browns a loss away from elimination, the decision was made to continue playing even if the Giants won their sixth game. New York did indeed clinch the series early, winning Game Eight 11-3 behind Keefe, who finished with 4 wins, 30 strikeouts, and an ERA of 0.51. The final games were played in Sportsman's Park as

Tim Keefe's four victories were the difference in the 1888 World Series.

Buck Ewing, the do-it-all star of the New York Giants

"exhibitions" and were won by the Browns. Once again, Von der Ahe cheated his players out of their share of the post-season money, claiming they had performed so badly against the Giants that they did not deserve it.

> **Giants 6**
> Best Players: Tim Keefe
> (4 W, 0.51 ERA);
> Buck Ewing (.615 SA)
> **Browns 4**
> Best Player: Tip O'Neill (11 RBIs)

1889
New York Giants (NL) vs. Brooklyn Bridegrooms (AA)

The Giants took the NL flag for the second year in a row behind the hard throwing of Tim Keefe and big seasons from John Ward, Buck Ewing, and Roger Connor. New York needed a win on the final day to clinch the pennant, and Keefe came through with a 5-3 victory over the Cleveland Blues. The American Association pennant went to the Brooklyn Bridegrooms, who ended the four-in-a-row pennant run of the Browns. Bob Caruthers, the AA's highest-paid player, and Adonis Terry manned the mound for Brooklyn, while Oyster Burns and pitcher-turned-outfielder Dave Foutz provided lusty hitting. The 1889 series marked the first postseason meeting of two teams from the same metropolitan area. A six-of-eleven format would be used again, but both sides agreed that the series would end when one team reached six victories—an important step in the evolution of the postseason format.

Brooklyn won Game One, a seesaw battle that was decided after darkness had fallen on the Polo Grounds. Umpire Bob Ferguson, a Brooklyn native, kept the game going until the Bridegrooms scored four runs in the eighth inning to pull ahead 12-10, then called it. Not surprisingly, Ferguson was replaced for Game Two, which drew a record 16,172 fans. The Giants won, as Cannonball Crane outpitched Caruthers in a 6-2 game. Games Three and Four went to Brooklyn, which grabbed late-inning leads and then shamelessly stalled until darkness forced the umpires to award them the victories. With the support of New York owner John Day, Ewing informed the Bridegrooms that the Giants planned to pull out of the series unless the nonsense ended.

Fearing a catastrophic financial loss, Brooklyn owner Charlie Byrne agreed to start the remaining games at 2:00 P.M. instead of 3:00. The rest of the series went smoothly—especially for Giants rooters, who watched their team reel off five straight wins to take the championship 6 games to 3.

The surprising part about New York's triumph was that pitching stars Keefe and Mickey Welch figured very little in these victories. New York's two best hurlers were clearly exhausted from the tight pennant race, so manager Jim Mutrie turned to Crane and Hank O'Day, who had a grand total of 23 victories between them. Crane won three of the last five, with O'Day pitching the Giants to triumphs in Games Six and Nine. Connor and Ward led the New York hitters with help from second baseman Danny Richardson, who hit three home runs and knocked in the run that won the championship.

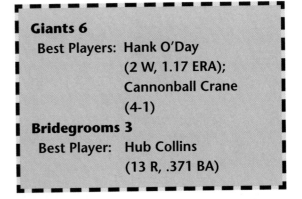

Giants 6
Best Players: Hank O'Day
(2 W, 1.17 ERA);
Cannonball Crane
(4-1)
Bridegrooms 3
Best Player: Hub Collins
(13 R, .371 BA)

1890
Brooklyn Bridegrooms (NL) vs. Louisville Cyclones (AA)

The Louisville Colonels, who had lost 111 games in 1889, figured it was time for a name change. In the early months of 1890, a killer tornado ripped through the city of Louisville and caused great property damage and loss of life. The Colonels decided to capitalize on this tragedy by memorializing its victims, and the Louisville Cyclones were born.

The Cyclones opened the American Association season without their best hitter, Pete Browning, who had jumped to the new Players League—a third major league set up by John Ward and other stars who wished to wrest control of baseball from the greedy owners. Because the Louisville Colonels had been playing so poorly, no one had "raided" their other players. As a result, they whipped through the schedule with a record of 88-44 to win the pennant by 10 games. Their star was Jimmy "Chicken" Wolf, a marvelously versatile player who led the league with a .363 average and knocked in 98 runs. Veteran Red Ehret went from 10-29 to 25-14, and 20-year-old Scott Stratton went from 3-13 to 34-14.

BEST TEAM LEFT OUT OF A WORLD SERIES: BOSTON REDS, 1890

Michael "King" Kelly was a key figure in the 1890 players' rebellion that created a third major league. His Boston Reds featured some of the greatest players of the era, but the team was not invited to participate in the World Series.

While the Brooklyn Bridegrooms and Louisville Cyclones were busy doing battle in baseball's world championship series, baseball's best team sat idle. The Players League (or "Brotherhood," as its members called it) played one spectacular season, outdrawing the National League and American Association by virtue of having the world's best players. The best of the best were the Boston Reds.

The Reds were managed by the famous King Kelly, who turned down a huge offer from the National League to join his fellow stars in their adventure. At 32, he was still a wonderful player. He hit .326 with plenty of power, stole 51 bases, and handled about two-thirds of the team's catching duties. At first base stood Dan Brouthers, who was the most feared hitter in all of baseball. At second was Joe Quinn, the first Australian major leaguer, who would go on to play for a total of 17 seasons. The third baseman, Billy Nash, was a powerful hitter and good fielder. A few years later, as a player-manager, he developed superstar Napoleon Lajoie. Arthur Irwin, who started for the NL champion Providence Grays in 1884, was the shortstop.

The Boston outfield featured Hardy Richardson. The former slugging star of the old Detroit Wolverines led the Players League with 146 RBIs. Stationed in centerfield was Tom Brown, who was born in Liverpool, England. He was fast and strong. The following year Brown would lead the NL in stolen bases, runs, hits, and triples. In rightfield was Harry Stovey, who is often credited with perfecting the modern feet-first slide. Stovey had a great arm, a powerful bat, and a gentlemanly manner that was rare in this period. Of all the 19th-century players who did not make the Baseball Hall of Fame, Stovey is unquestionably the most deserving.

The Boston pitching staff featured the great Hoss Radbourn, who was coming to the end of the line. He went 27-12 for the Reds, leaving him two wins shy of 300 for his career. Ad Gumpert, the team's other primary starter, won 23 games at the age of 21. The two backup starters were Bill Daley and Matt Kilroy. Daley had the distinction of playing for all three of Boston's major-league teams during his three years in the major leagues. His 18-7 mark in 1890 gave him the second-highest winning percentage (.720) in all of baseball. Kilroy, who four years earlier had struck out an amazing 513 batters, was washed up by 1890 but still a crowd favorite.

The Boston Reds finished with a record of 81-48. They beat out Ward's Wonders of Brooklyn, the New York Giants, and the Chicago Pirates, who had been picked by many to win the pennant before the season started. The Players League disbanded after the 1890 season, when several owners were unable to meet their payrolls. Had the Brotherhood weathered the storm and played in 1891, it would have sunk the American Association and, in time, perhaps even would have overshadowed the National League. That is how much talent the Players League had.

The Bridegrooms repeated as champs, but they did so in the National League after transferring the franchise from the American Association over the winter (in much the same way that the Milwaukee Brewers switched leagues in 1998, nearly a century later). Brooklyn's roster was essentially the same, with the notable rise of Tom Lovett from mop-up man to 30-game winner. A best-of-nine format was agreed upon for the 1890 series. There was only lukewarm fan interest in the series, however, for the best players in the NL and AA were simply not the equals of those in the Players League, which was not invited to participate in the postseason.

The first four games of this unpromising World Series were held in Louisville. Adonis Terry hurled a marvelous two-hitter against the home team to win the opener 9-0. Game Two went to Lovett and the Bridegrooms 5-3, but the Louisville bats awoke two days later to earn a 7-7 tie before Game Three was called on account of darkness. The fourth and final game in Louisville was captured by the suddenly confident Cyclones, who rallied to break a 4-4 tie in the seventh for their first victory of the series.

Travel and poor weather delayed the series for four days. When it resumed, Brooklyn fans watched as their team trounced the Cyclones 7-2. The next game, which was played on a raw and frigid afternoon before fewer than 700 fans, featured the best hitting of the series. The teams combined for 25 hits, and Louisville won 9-8. Game Seven went to the Cyclones and knotted the series at 3-3-1. The weather had gotten so bad, the players so sick, and attendance so poor that the teams agreed to finish the series in the spring.

> **Cyclones 3**
>   Best Player: Red Ehret
>   (2-0, 1.35 ERA)
> **Bridegrooms 3**
>   Best Player: Germany Smith
>   (7 RBIs)
> **1 Tie**

Unfortunately, this never happened. The Players League folded over the winter, igniting squabbles between the NL and AA over returning players. The friction made it impossible to break the tie of the previous fall. A year later, the AA was dead, too, and for the next nine seasons, there was just one major league.

In 1892, the National League played a split season, and the winner of the first half (Boston Beaneaters) met the winner of the second half (Cleveland Spiders) in a "Pennant Series," which Boston won 5 games to 0. Baseball fans did not approve of this format, and it was a financial failure. At the end of the 1893 season, there was no championship series. At baseball's annual winter meetings that December, William Temple, former president of the Pittsburgh Pirates, suggested that the first- and second-place clubs play a title series at the end of each year. The owners agreed to try the idea, and Temple donated a large silver cup for the event.

The 1894 Temple Cup championship went to the Giants in a four-game sweep over the Baltimore Orioles. The Orioles, who had finished three games ahead of the Giants during the regular season, were still considered National League champions. More than 50,000 fans turned out to witness the four games, so the NL kept the Temple Cup going. In 1895, the Orioles played the

Cleveland Spiders. The Spiders, who had finished second to the Orioles in the regular season, won the series 4 games to 1.

After Baltimore's loss, interest in the Temple Cup began to decline. Most baseball fans still considered the pennant-winning Orioles the league champs. What sense did it make to play a postseason championship when the loser was still regarded as champion? After the Orioles won their third pennant and then swept the Spiders 4 games to 0 in 1896, there was even less fan support for the series.

The Orioles missed a fourth consecutive pennant in 1897 but then beat the first-place Boston Beaneaters 4 games to 1 in the Temple Cup. Won by the second-place club three times in four seasons, the Temple Cup had lost all fan support. In November 1897, the owners officially let it die.

In 1900, the Western League—a minor league that had grown in stature during the 1890s—placed teams into several National League cities and renamed itself the American League (AL). In 1901, the AL announced its desire for major-league status. When the NL ignored this demand, the AL plundered NL rosters and drove salaries sky-high. Seeing quickly that a war would not do either league any good, they agreed to work side by side beginning in 1903.

Immediately, fans began clamoring for a new World Series. It had been more than ten years since an October series had decided baseball's true champion, and here was a perfect opportunity to revive this tradition. Most of the NL owners, still furious at their AL counterparts, were against the idea. Luckily, Barney Dreyfuss, owner of the pennant-winning Pittsburgh Pirates, saw things differently. A "World's Series" sounded like a grand scheme to him. By late summer, the arrangements were made for a best-of-nine postseason playoff for the "world championship."

CHAPTER 2

1903–1909

1903
Pittsburgh Pirates (NL)
vs. Boston Pilgrims (AL)

Even today, the Pirates stand as one of the most talented ball clubs in history. In 1903, shortstop Honus Wagner, player-manager Fred Clarke, slugger Tommy Leach, and leadoff man Ginger Beaumont ranked among the game's top hitters, while the starting trio of Deacon Phillippe, Sam Leever, and Ed Doheny combined for 65 wins. The Pilgrims had the AL's best pitching staff, with 20-game winners Cy Young, Bill Dinneen, and Long Tom Hughes. Boston's offense was powered by outfielders Buck Freeman and Patsy Dougherty and player-manager Jimmy Collins. Looking back, it is clear that nagging injuries to several Pirates—including Wagner and Leever—gave Boston a slight edge. At the time, however, most fans outside of Boston assumed that the Pirates would smash the AL champs.

The Pirates jumped on Young for four 2-out runs in the first inning of the opener. Phillippe held that margin of victory for a 7-3 win. Leever, whose shoulder had been injured during a trapshooting contest, lasted just one inning in Game Two. Dougherty drove one of his first deliveries into deep right-centerfield and circled the bases, providing all the scoring Dinneen needed in a 3-0 shutout that tied the series. Game Three saw Clarke send Phillippe back to the mound. The Deacon threw well again, winning 4-2. The Pirates took a 3 games to 1 series lead three days later when Phillippe won yet again, 5-3.

Cy Young's graceful, easy delivery produced a fastball that handcuffed enemy hitters. He won twice in the 1903 World Series.

Fans pack the grandstand and ring the outfield prior to a 1903 World Series game at the Huntington Avenue grounds in Boston. Spectators surrounding the infield had to move back once the game started.

Hoping to squeeze a win out of someone else on his staff, Clarke started veteran Brickyard Kennedy. He and Young traded outs for five innings, but the Pittsburgh defense fell apart in the sixth and so did Kennedy, who left the game down 10-0. Boston went on to win 11-2 and then captured Game Six 6-3. A rainout gave Phillippe an extra day of rest before he took the mound for Game Seven. Unfortunately for the Pirates, one day was not enough. Boston won again, 7-3, and returned home up 4 games to 3. Two travel days and a rainout gave both managers a chance to handpick their starters. Collins selected the well-rested Dinneen. Clarke tabbed the exhausted Phillippe again and hoped for the best. Phillippe pitched marvelously, giving up just two earned runs, but Dinneen twirled a four-hitter to give Boston the championship, 3-0.

Pilgrims 5
Best Players: Bill Dinneen (3 W);
Cy Young
(2 W, 1.85 ERA)
Pirates 3
Best Player: Deacon Phillippe
(5 GS, 3 W)

1904
No World Series Held

The Pilgrims were denied a chance to defend their world title in 1904, when manager John McGraw of the pennant-winning Giants refused to let his team play in what was still technically an exhibition series. McGraw felt he had been double-crossed by American League president Ban Johnson two years earlier. Refusing to play in the postseason was his revenge.

The AL planned to move the Baltimore Orioles into New York City for the 1903 season. McGraw, who was Baltimore's manager and part-owner, stood to profit handsomely from his stake in the new team, which would eventually become the Yankees. However, McGraw's vicious umpire-baiting during the 1902 season had become such an embarrassment to the AL

that Johnson suspended him indefinitely that July.

Enraged, McGraw put together a deal that enabled National League executive (and Giants president) John Brush to buy the Orioles. Brush then released all of the Orioles' key players, including McGraw, and they all signed with NL teams. Overnight, the Orioles went from being one of the better teams in the AL to being unable to field a team. McGraw ended up on

BEST SERIES BY A PITCHER: CHRISTY MATHEWSON, 1905

The most games won by a pitcher in a World Series is three. Between 1903 and 2000, a dozen hurlers accomplished this feat—but no one ever did it better than Christy Mathewson. In the 1905 series against the Philadelphia Athletics, "Matty" started three times and threw three complete-game shutouts. You simply cannot pitch any better than that.

Mathewson was very different from the other players of his time. The son of a gentleman farmer, he had attended Bucknell University in Pennsylvania, where he was voted class president and was the star of the football team. He loved the science of pitching and even wrote a book on the subject. Mathewson's best pitch was the "fade-away," which looked like a fastball but curved and dipped in on the fists of right-handed batters. The pitch put a tremendous strain on his arm, so he only threw it once or twice an inning, but batters were always on the lookout for it. This made his fastball, curve, and sinker all the more effective.

Like most pitchers at the turn of the twentieth century, Mathewson did not try to strike hitters out unless it was absolutely necessary. The ball used back then did not carry very well, so it was to his advantage to make opponents swing and hit rather than swing and miss. Mathewson's genius was that he rarely threw the pitch a batter was expecting.

Originally signed by the New York Giants in 1900, Mathewson was returned to the minors after losing his first three games. The Cincinnati Reds signed him after that and then traded him back to the Giants for old-timer Amos Rusie. The trade the last-place Giants, where he played shortstop and took over managerial duties. After guiding the team to a 24-win improvement in 1903, he won the league in 1904 by a remarkable 13 games over the Chicago Cubs. The chance to burn Johnson again by not participating in the World Series was too delicious to pass up. McGraw called the Pilgrims "bush leaguers" and simply refused to accept their challenge.

1905
New York Giants (NL) vs. Philadelphia Athletics (AL)

The World Series was officially adopted as baseball's best-of-seven championship in 1905, so John McGraw had no choice but to play the AL champions when the Giants finished first again. New York boasted great pitching, led by young Christy Mathewson

was made because Cincinnati's owner, John T. Brush, planned to buy the Giants (which he did in 1902), and he was convinced that the young right-hander would be a star. Mathewson won 20 games in 1901 and led the National League with eight shutouts in 1902. He won 30 games in 1903, then led the Giants to the pennant with 33 victories in 1904. By 1905, when he led the NL with 31 wins, Mathewson was hailed as baseball's best pitcher.

Still, no one could have imagined he would do what he did during the World Series that year. In the opener, Mathewson gave up only four hits in a 3-0 victory. He also helped himself in the field, pouncing on a suicide-squeeze bunt and shoveling the ball to catcher Roger Bresnahan in time to tag the runner out. In Game Three, with the series tied 1-1, Mathewson gave up just four hits and struck out eight in a 9-0 victory. Again he made key plays in the field, trapping a runner off second in the second inning and snaring a hot grounder in the fourth.

After teammate Joe McGinnity won Game Four (also a shutout!), the Athletics had one more crack at Matty. For Philadelphia, scoring some runs off the Giants' star was now a matter of pride. Connie Mack's hitters were the finest in the American League, leading everyone in batting, slugging, runs, and doubles. First baseman Harry Davis was a big star; he had managed just two hits off Mathewson. Topsy Hartsell was the best leadoff man in the game; he had reached base just once in eight tries. The two players finally broke through in Game Five, going three for eight. But the rest of the team got just two more hits, as Mathewson allowed a total of five and was never in any serious trouble. In fact, the only problem he had was with his own fielding. Twice he fumbled grounders he should have fielded cleanly. Mathewson made up for his mistakes at the plate, where he walked and scored the insurance run in a 2-0 win.

Mathewson's stats for the series were 27 innings pitched, 14 hits, 18 strikeouts, only one walk—and an ERA of 0.00.

and veteran Joe McGinnity. Hard-hitting Dan McGann, Mike Donlin, Sam Mertes, and catcher Roger Bresnahan, the team's leadoff hitter, provided New York's offensive punch.

The Philadelphia A's had streaked past the White Sox in August and held on to win the AL pennant by two games. The A's did not have an imposing lineup, but their pitching was terrific. Rube Waddell, Eddie Plank, Chief Bender, and Andy Coakley won a total of 87 times, although Waddell was hurt and unavailable for the series.

There was little mystery to this series. The Giants had better hitting and pitching and were the more aggressive team. No one could have predicted how decisively they would win, however. Game One featured a four-hit shutout by Mathewson, with Donlin, Mertes, and Bresnahan getting clutch RBIs for a 3-0 victory. Bender evened the series the next afternoon, blanking the Giants 3-0 with a four-hitter of his own. Not to be outdone, Mathewson pitched another four-hit shutout in Game Three as the Giants smoked Coakley for nine runs.

Up 2 games to 1, McGraw started McGinnity against Plank and was rewarded with a 1-0 shutout. With four straight shutouts pitched, the fans at New York's Polo Grounds had every right to expect a fifth whitewash. To their delight, the final blow was delivered by Mathewson, who scored the insurance run in a 2-0 victory that gave the Giants their first true championship since 1889. Five games, five shutouts—the World Series would never see pitching like this again. No hurler would ever repeat Mathewson's eye-popping performance.

Giants 4
Best Players: Christy Mathewson
(3 shutouts);
Billy Gilbert
(GW RBIs in
Games 4 and 5)
Athletics 1
Best Player: Bris Lord
(2 RBIs in Game 2 W)

1906
Chicago Cubs (NL) vs. Chicago White Sox (AL)

Although the World Series is meant to be a meeting of league champions, occasionally the talent gap between the two clubs is so great that the series takes on a David vs. Goliath flavor. The first such battle took place in 1906, when the Chicago Cubs—winners of 116 games—took on their crosstown rivals, the Chicago White Sox. On paper, the Sox had no right to be on the same field. The team's .228 batting average was not only appalling, it was the second worst in the majors. Adding to the woes of the "Hitless Wonders"—as they were called in the Chicago papers—was the fact that their strongest batter, shortstop George Davis, was not at full strength when the series started. The Sox pitching staff was good but not great. It featured Frank Owen, Nick Altrock, Doc White, and Ed Walsh, who at 25 became the first person to truly master the erratic (and, in 1906, legal) spitball.

The Cubs, on the other hand, were really scary. They had won the pennant by 20 games. Their lineup boasted some of the greatest hitters of the day—Frank Chance,

Johnny Evers, Joe Tinker, Wildfire Schulte, Jimmy Sheckard, and Harry Steinfeldt. The mound corps included Mordecai "Three-Finger" Brown, Jack Pfiester, Ed Reulbach, and Orvie Overall, whose combined winning percentage was a phenomenal .786.

Altrock and Brown faced each other in the opener, which was played amidst snow flurries. The White Sox prevailed 2-1 in an exciting game that featured a booming triple by shortstop George Rohe, who was subbing for Davis. The weather was even worse the next day, when Reulbach one-hit the White Sox and Tinker and Steinfeldt led the Cubs to a 7-1 win. Game Three featured a pitching duel between Walsh and Pfiester. Once again, the difference in the game was Rohe, whose bases-loaded triple accounted for all the runs in a 3-0 White Sox victory. The Cubs battled back in Game Four, with Brown striking out 12 and giving up just two hits in a 1-0 shutout.

The cold weather finally broke for Game Five, and all of Chicago came to the game. The overflow fans were seated inside the outfield fences, which cut down the outfield space dramatically. This led to a record 11 doubles, as ball after ball rolled into the crowd for ground-rule two-base hits. The White Sox turned an early 3-1 deficit into a 7-3 lead in the fourth inning and then held on to win 8-6. Second baseman Cecil Isbell stroked four doubles in the game. Hoping to stave off elimination, Frank Chance sent a tired Brown back to the mound. The Sox exploded for seven runs in the first two innings. White limited the Cubs to three runs, and the battle of Chicago went to the underdog White Sox, who ended up out-hitting the Cubs—.198 to .196!

White Sox 4
Best Players: Ed Walsh (2-0, 17 K);
George Rohe (.571 SA)
Cubs 2
Best Player: Jack Pfiester
(3 ER in 2 starts)

1907
Chicago Cubs (NL)
vs. Detroit Tigers (AL)

No one was surprised to see the Cubs back in the World Series. Once again, they ran away with the NL pennant, this time by 17 games. The Chicago pitching staff was even deeper in 1907 than it was in 1906, while Harry Steinfeldt, Johnny Evers, and Jimmy Sheckard had huge years at the plate. The Tigers were a team on the rise. From sixth place in 1906, they had climbed into a spirited four-way pennant race with the Athletics, the White Sox, and the Cleveland Naps. The Tigers took the AL flag after pulling ahead of the A's on September 27. The Detroit offense featured the league's two strongest hitters, slugger Sam Crawford and a 20-year-old whirlwind named Ty Cobb. Cobb led the American League with a .350 average, 49 stolen bases, and 119 RBIs. The starting four of Wild Bill Donovan, Ed Killian, George Mullin, and Ed Siever accounted for all but three of the Tigers' 92 wins.

Cub fans watched in frustration as their team fell behind 3-1 in the opener but cheered wildly when Chicago tied the game in the bottom of the ninth on a dropped third strike by Detroit catcher Boss Schmidt. The teams played for three more innings before it was too dark to see and the game was called. Jack Pfiester took the mound for Game Two and allowed just one Tiger run in a 3-1 victory; then Ed Reulbach scattered six Detroit hits to win Game Three 5-1.

The series shifted to Detroit, where drizzle and a two-game deficit combined to hold attendance down to 11,000. A tight ballgame blew up in the Tigers' faces when the Cubs scored three runs in the eighth without getting a ball out of the infield. Orvie Overall pitched a whale of a game and picked up the 6-1 decision. The Tigers went quietly the next afternoon, as Three-Finger Brown twirled a 2-0 shutout.

Cubs 4
Best Players: Ed Reulbach
(2 GS, 0.75 ERA);
Harry Steinfeldt (.471 BA)
Tigers 0
Best Player: Claude Rossman
(.400 BA)
1 Tie

1908
Chicago Cubs (NL) vs. Detroit Tigers (AL)

This rematch of the 1907 World Series featured a nearly identical cast of characters. Sam Crawford, Ty Cobb, and Claude Rossman did the bulk of the hitting for Detroit. For Chicago, Frank Chance, Johnny Evers, and shortstop Joe Tinker, who had developed into a formidable run producer, anchored an all-around speedy lineup. Of course, like most short series of this era, pitching was expected to be the key. Here the Cubs had the edge once again, with stars Three-Finger Brown, Ed Reulbach, Orvie Overall, and Jack Pfiester. The Tigers countered with a less talented staff but hoped that rookie knuckleballer Ed Summers—a surprise 24-game winner—would give them the boost they needed to get their revenge on the Chicagoans.

Game One saw the Cubs knock Ed Killian out early, but Summers entered in the third inning and managed to hold Chicago in

This score-card from the 1908 World Series depicts Detroit's best player, Ty Cobb.

PRICE 10 CENTS

PENNANT WINNERS

WORLD'S CHAMPIONSHIP SERIES

OFFICIAL SCORE CARD

DETROIT "TIGERS"
AMERICAN LEAGUE
VS.
CHICAGO "CUBS"
NATIONAL LEAGUE

BENNETT PARK, DETROIT, OCTOBER 1908

H. M. FECHHEIMER, PUBLISHER, 108 WOODWARD AVE.

check. Meanwhile, Cobb and Rossman led a charge that gave the Tigers a 6-5 lead heading into the top of the ninth. Then Summers allowed six straight singles, and the Cubs won 10-6. The pitchers took over the next day, as Wild Bill Donovan and Overall took a scoreless game into the eighth inning. Tinker broke things open with a wind-blown opposite-field home run, and the Cubs went on to win 6-1.

The Tigers' bats awoke in Game Three against Pfiester, with Cobb collecting four hits in an 8-3 blowout. With the series moving back to Detroit, there was a ray of hope for the Tigers. But Brown was at his best in Game Four, outdueling Summers and keeping the ball down during a game in which 26 of 27 Tiger outs came on either grounders or strikeouts. The Cubs won 3-0, then finished off Detroit the next day on Overall's second complete-game win of the series. The Tigers, unable to get anyone on base after Cobb's leadoff walk in the sixth inning, lost 2-0. On this raw October Wednesday in Detroit, fewer than 6,500 fans watched as the Cubs celebrated their second straight world title.

> **Cubs 4**
> Best Players: Orvie Overall (2 W);
> Frank Chance (.421 BA,
> 5 SB, winning H)
> **Tigers 1**
> Best Player: Ty Cobb (.368 BA)

1909
Pittsburgh Pirates (NL) vs. Detroit Tigers (AL)

Lost in Chicago's three straight pennant wins from 1906 to 1908 was the fine play of the Pittsburgh Pirates, who always found a way

to win around 90 games. In 1909, the "Bucs" found a way to win 110, which was too much for the slow-starting Cubs to overcome. The Pirate offense still revolved around Honus Wagner, whose .339 average was good for his fourth straight batting crown. Outfielder Tommy Leach, rookie infielder Dots Miller, and player-manager Fred Clarke also had fine seasons at the plate. Pitcher Vic Willis chalked up 22 wins, second on the staff to Howie Camnitz's 25, while Nick Maddox, Babe Adams, and Lefty Leifield rounded out a formidable staff. The Tigers had three significant new faces in the lineup: first baseman Tom Jones, second baseman Jim

Honus Wagner, the top player in the National League

Delehanty (picked up in summer trades), and George Moriarty, a speedy third baseman. George Mullin led the league with 29 wins; Ed Summers chipped in 19; and Wild Bill Donovan, now 32, struggled to win eight games. Sam Crawford and Ty Cobb still powered the offense, as Cobb approached the peak of his skills. In 1909, the "Georgia Peach" won the AL Triple Crown and also finished first in runs, hits, stolen bases, and slugging percentage.

The two best players in baseball, Wagner and Cobb, were the focus of the series, which promised to feature plenty of daring base running. Adams yielded a run to the Tigers in the first inning of Game One, but then settled down and allowed just four hits the rest of the way for a 4-1 win. Detroit bounced back 7-2 a day later, as Donovan found his old form, Cobb stole home, and catcher Boss Schmidt knocked in four runs. The series moved to Detroit, where the Pirates jumped all over Summers in an 8-6 slugfest that saw Wagner get three hits and steal three bases. The Tigers knotted the series when Mullin fanned ten in a brilliant 5-0 shutout.

Game Five, in Pittsburgh, was a must-win for the Pirates, for the final two games were scheduled for Detroit. The Pirates cracked open a 3-3 game in the seventh inning on a three-run homer to centerfield by Clarke, then went on to win 8-4. For the third time in three years, Detroit was staring elimination in the face. But this time the Tigers hung tough, taking Game Six 5-4 in an exciting battle. For Game Seven, Clarke bypassed his Big Three starters and went with Adams, who had already won twice. The Tigers sent Donovan to the mound. Adams was brilliant, blanking Detroit on six hits, while the Pirates roughed up Donovan and Mullin, who relieved in the fourth. The final score was 8-0. The Tigers, one of history's best teams, had blown it yet again.

Ty Cobb's poor series against the Pirates did little to tarnish his image as baseball's dominant player.

Pirates 4
Best Players: Babe Adams
(3 W, 1.33 ERA);
Honus Wagner
(6 SB, 6 RBIs)
Tigers 3
Best Player: George Mullin
(32 IP, 2 W)

CHAPTER 3

THE 1910s

1910
Chicago Cubs (NL) vs.
Philadelphia Athletics (AL)

Connie Mack knew how to build a baseball team. His 1910 pennant winners were proof of that. To a nucleus of players from the 1905 team—Danny Murphy, Harry Davis, Topsy Hartsell, Chief Bender, and Eddie Plank—he added the talented young cast of slugger Frank Baker, lightning-fast Eddie Collins, and right-handed starter Jack Coombs, a college kid who pitched a remarkable 13 shutouts on his way to 31 wins in 1910. The Cubs returned to the World Series for the fourth time in five years, led again by the pitching of Three-Finger Brown and the all-around great play of Johnny Evers, who had battled back from a nervous breakdown suffered the year before.

The A's jumped out to an early three-run lead in Game One, with Baker getting a pair of key hits. Bender allowed just three singles in a 4-1 win. Game Two saw Brown get

The 1910 Cubs, with player-manager Frank Chance front and center, were an imposing team—but they were no match for A's pitcher Jack Coombs.

BEST NICKNAME:
HOME RUN BAKER, 1911

In the early years of baseball, third basemen were prized for one skill—defense. Fielding hot shots and bunts and making the long throw to first basemen wearing tiny gloves were considered near-impossible tasks. There had been a few heavy hitters at third. Ned Williamson of Chicago was perhaps the most notable. The first great all-around third sacker was Jimmy Collins of the Boston Beaneaters and later the Boston Pilgrims. He positioned himself differently depending on the batter, the count, and the situation, and he perfected the barehanded pickup and throw now taught to every third baseman. Collins could also hit.

The heir to Collins's throne as king of the third basemen was up for grabs in 1911. Larry Gardner of the Red Sox and Hans Lobert of the Phillies could hit but were only average fielders. Jimmy Austin of the Browns and Eddie Grant of the Reds were good fielders but just average hitters. Frank Baker, who joined Connie Mack's Philadelphia Athletics in 1908, was as good a hitter as anyone had seen at the position, but his fielding was inconsistent. Baker was just 24 when the Athletics won the World Series in 1910. He hit well and fielded poorly in Philadelphia's five-game victory over the Cubs, but no one really noticed him. In 1911, however, Baker came into his own. He led the league in home runs, tied for second with 115 RBIs, and was the AL's top fielder. Suddenly recognized as baseball's best third baseman, all Baker needed to cement his place in history was a nickname.

The opportunity came during the 1911 World Series against the New York Giants. With the Giants leading the series 1 game to 0, and the score tied in the sixth inning of Game Two, Baker came to the plate against Rube Marquard. Marquard was not in the habit of making bad pitches in tight games. With a man on second and Baker looking for a ball he could drive, the Giants' hurler threw one up and in. Baker leaned back, whipped his bat around, and caught the pitch perfectly. The Philadelphia fans rose in unison as the ball soared toward rightfield. Red Murray gave chase for a step or two, but then, realizing that the ball was headed over the wall, stopped to watch with the 26,000 other occupants of the ballpark. The Athletics won 3-1, and the next morning the Game Two hero was being called "Home Run" Baker in the Philadelphia papers. In the New York papers, Marquard was being criticized for his pitch selection by teammate Christy Mathewson, who had been hired to write a daily column.

In Game Three, Mathewson was on the mound for the Giants, pitching his usual masterful game. Ahead 1-0 in the ninth inning, Matty retired Eddie Collins on a grounder. Baker, whom he had retired easily three times, stepped into the batter's box. Mathewson reared back and fired his best fastball. Baker swung right through

Frank Baker earned his nickname with quick hands and a whopping 52-ounce bat.

it. He refused to offer at two pitches off the plate, and the count became two and one. Mathewson now had to give him something decent to hit. But which of his many fine pitches would it be? Deciding he would take another fastball if Mathewson threw it, Baker waited for the famous "fade-away." The pitch started inside, but Baker could see from its rotation that he had guessed correctly, and he stepped into it. As the pitch darted over the plate, he started his massive 52-ounce (1.5-kg) bat on its trip through the strike zone and caught the fade-away just as it crossed over the heart of the plate. Once again, Murray could do nothing but watch the ball sail over the fence. The score was tied, and so it remained until the 11th inning, when Collins and Baker reached base. A bad throw, a fielding error, and a clean single scored both men, and the Athletics went on to win 3-2. The next morning Marquard, who had also been hired to pen his opinions on the World Series, had some interesting things to say about Mathewson.

Home Run Baker's place in history was now assured. The Athletics took two of the next three games (Baker got four important hits in the two victories) to win their second straight championship. Baker would lead the American League in round-trippers three more times, help Philadelphia win two more pennants, and provide veteran leadership for the Yankees during their pennants in 1921 and 1922. When he retired, he was considered the best all-around third baseman in history. But even if his two World Series home runs had been his last, Baker would have kept that nickname forever.

shelled by Philadelphia, as Collins got three hits and stole two bases in a 9-3 victory. In Game Three, the A's beat up on Chicago again, this time victimizing Ed Reulbach, Harry McIntire, and Jack Pfiester. Murphy broke open a close game with a three-run homer in the third, and Coombs picked up his second win by a score of 12-5.

The Cubs avoided a sweep in thrilling fashion, as they tied Game Four 3-3 on a ninth-inning triple by Frank Chance and won it in the tenth when Jimmy Sheckard laced a two-out single to centerfield off Bender. A day later it was all over, however, as Philadelphia exploded for five runs in the eighth off Brown to win 7-2. The overwhelming victory by Philadelphia was a changing of the guard. The A's were beginning a reign of terror over the American League, while it would take an eight-year rebuilding effort before the Cubs would reclaim the National League pennant.

Athletics 4
  Best Players: Jack Coombs (3 W);
               Danny Murphy
               (.650 SA, 9 RBIs)
Cubs 1
  Best Player: Frank Chance
               (.353, 4 RBIs)

1911
New York Giants (NL) vs. Philadelphia Athletics (AL)

Two baseball legends were born in 1911. Connie Mack unveiled his "$100,000 Infield" of Stuffy McInnis, Eddie Collins, Jack Barry, and Frank Baker—nicknamed for the astronomical figure representing their value on the open market. The other legend was born during the World Series, when Baker flashed the power that had enabled him to lead the American League in home runs that year. The A's returned to the series with the same group that had gotten them there in 1910, including pitchers Jack Coombs, Chief Bender, and Eddie Plank.

Their opponents, the New York Giants, had finally figured out the Cubs. They finished 7.5 games ahead of Chicago. John McGraw's team was built on speed, pitching, and defense. Fred Merkle, Larry Doyle, Fred Snodgrass, Josh Devore, and Red Murray—all between the ages of 22 and 27—averaged 50 steals apiece. Veteran Christy Mathewson and a hard-throwing youngster named Rube Marquard were the staff's big winners.

Mathewson and Bender, who last tangled in the finale of the 1905 World Series, turned back the clock and allowed just 11 hits between them. A run-scoring double by Devore was the difference in a 2-1 New York victory. Game Two also featured a 1-1 tie, but this time Philadelphia broke it. In the sixth inning, with Collins on second, Baker leaned into a Marquard delivery and smashed a home run over the rightfield wall for a 3-1 win. Baker struck again in the ninth inning of Game Three. With one out and his team trailing 1-0, he took Mathewson deep to force extra innings. The Giants bobbled a couple of balls in the 11th and lost 3-2. The next morning, newspapers were trumpeting the exploits of baseball's newest superstar, "Home Run" Baker.

Six days of rain delayed the start of Game Four, which found Mathewson on the mound for New York once again. Baker doubled in the fourth and fifth innings to spark the A's to a 4-2 lead, and Bender blanked the

Giants the rest of the way to give his team a 3 games to 1 edge. Their backs against the wall, the Giants put up a marvelous fight before 33,000 fans at the Polo Grounds. Down 3-1 in the ninth with two out, they rallied to tie the game and won it in the tenth. The series returned to Philadelphia, where the Athletics unloaded on veterans Red Ames and Hooks Wiltse in a 13-2 blowout.

Athletics 4
Best Players: Frank Baker
(2 HR, .708 SA);
Chief Bender
(2 W, 20 K)
Giants 2
Best Player: Larry Doyle (.522 SA)

John McGraw's fleet-footed outfielders: (left to right) Fred Snodgrass, Josh Devore, Red Murray, and Beals Becker. They swiped 179 bases in 1911 and 138 bases in 1912.

1912
New York Giants (NL) vs. Boston Red Sox (AL)

Pitching and defense were the keys to success in baseball's Dead Ball Era, and the 1912 Red Sox—winners of 105 games—defined this lethal combination. Smokey Joe Wood, just 22 years old, blossomed into the AL's top right-hander with 34 wins and 10 shutouts. The Boston outfield trio of Duffy Lewis, Tris Speaker, and Harry Hooper was easily the best defensive unit the game had ever seen. Their October opponents, the Giants, had a great pitching staff, too. And what they lacked in power, they made up for with speed and daring on the bases. As in 1911, Christy Mathewson and Rube Marquard would be counted upon to do the bulk of the postseason mound work.

Hoping to shake up the Red Sox, John McGraw started scatter-armed rookie Jeff Tesreau in the opener. It looked like a bright move until Boston got four hits in the seventh inning to turn a 2-1 deficit into a 4-3 win for Wood, who fanned 11. Mathewson started Game Two, but his gritty 11-inning performance went to waste in a 6-6 tie. Marquard got his team even with a 2-1 victory in Game Three to send the series back to New York, where, to the frustration of the fans, the Red Sox took a commanding lead by winning the next two games. Wood pitched brilliantly to take Game Four, and Hugh Bedient shut down the Giants and beat Mathewson in Game Five 2-1, allowing just three hits.

New York finally got in gear in Game Six. A couple of infield singles, a couple of long hits, and a double steal produced five runs in the first inning, and Marquard did

the rest in a 5-2 victory. Game Seven, back in Boston, saw the Giants strike early again with six first-inning runs for an 11-5 win to set up a winner-take-all Game Eight. It was a classic, with Mathewson up against Bedient and Wood. After nine innings, the score was tied 1-1. In the tenth, Fred Merkle singled home Red Murray to put the Giants ahead. In the bottom of the tenth, Boston pinch hitter Clyde Engle hit a soft fly to centerfielder Fred Snodgrass, who dropped the ball. Hooper then blasted what looked to be a certain extra-base hit, but Snodgrass made a brilliant lunging grab. After his foul pop-up was misplayed, Speaker singled home Engle. One batter later, the bases were loaded. Lefty Larry Gardner pulled a Mathewson pitch deep to rightfield, and the winning run trotted home on a sacrifice fly.

Red Sox 4
Best Players: Joe Wood (3-1); Tris Speaker (.467 SA)
Giants 3
Best Player: Rube Marquard (2-0, 0.50 ERA)
1 Tie

1913
New York Giants (NL) vs. Philadelphia Athletics (AL)

New York manager John McGraw sought to end his two-year World Series losing streak against a club that had changed little since they last met in 1911. Slugger Frank Baker and fleet-footed Eddie Collins still powered the Philadelphia offense, while Chief Bender and Eddie Plank were the big names on the pitching staff. The great Jack Coombs, however, had fallen ill. His place in the rotation went to a hard-throwing 20-year-old named Bullet Joe Bush. After running away with the NL pennant, the Giants came into the series bruised and battered. Their two Freds—Snodgrass and Merkle—were hobbling on sore legs, sapping the lineup of its main strength, team speed. New York's only hope was that its three 20-game winners—veterans Christy Mathewson and Rube Marquard and young spitballer Jeff Tesreau—would muffle the Philadelphia offense.

The opener featured lusty hitting by both teams, and Home Run Baker lived up to his nickname once again. With Collins dancing off second base, Baker blasted a Marquard pitch into the rightfield stands for the decisive blow in a 6-4 Philadelphia victory. Prior to the second game, New York catcher Chief Meyers broke a finger during warm-ups; McGraw's lone .300 hitter was now gone for the rest of the series. Mathewson brightened the Giants' prospects when he stepped up and blanked the A's for 10 innings and singled in the winning run in a 3-0 victory. Pitcher George Wiltse, playing first base for the injured Merkle, earned an unofficial "save" when he gunned down two runners trying to score on ground balls in a wild ninth inning.

Unfortunately for the Giants, Game Two was the highlight of the series. In Game Three, the A's ran wild on Tesreau and substitute catcher Larry McLean to win 8-2 behind the five-hit pitching of Bush. Bush's unexpected victory meant Mack could finish off the Giants with Bender and Plank. Bender outlasted Al DeMaree and Marquard in a 6-5 Philadelphia triumph, and Plank got the better of Mathewson in

Game Five to deliver the world championship to the Mackmen.

> **Athletics 4**
> Best Players: Frank Baker
> (.450 BA, 7 RBIs);
> Chief Bender (2 W)
> **Giants 1**
> Best Player: Christy Mathewson
> (2 ER in 19 IP)

1914
Boston Braves (NL) vs. Philadelphia Athletics (AL)

Connie Mack's "$100,000 Infield" of Stuffy McInnis, Eddie Collins, Jack Barry, and Home Run Baker produced a third pennant in four years with help from a pitching staff that combined the live young arms of Bullet Joe Bush, Bob Shawkey, and Herb Pennock with veterans Eddie Plank and Chief Bender. This awesome team faced the "Miracle Braves," who climbed from last place in mid-July to win the NL pennant. They did so with great defense and clutch hitting from infielders Johnny Evers and Rabbit Maranville, brilliant platooning by manager George Stallings, and a three-man pitching staff that was practically unbeatable during the second half of the season. Bill James, Dick Rudolph, and Lefty Tyler won a total of 68 times, and at season's end, the Braves were a miraculous 10.5 games ahead of the second-place Giants. Still, no one expected Boston to take more than a game or two from the A's in the World Series.

As history has proved many times since the 1914 World Series, a weird team like the

Miracle Braves manager George Stallings is flanked by his two aces, Bill James (left) and Dick Rudolph (right). The Braves went 52-17 during the 1914 season.

hop on his fastball, and he dominated the A's in a two-hit shutout.

Game Three saw Bush and Tyler go into extra innings tied 2-2. The A's seemed to lock it up in the tenth on a two-run single by Baker, but the relentless Braves tied the score on a home run and sacrifice fly. Two innings later, Boston won the game when Bush fielded a bunt and threw the ball away. Again, Gowdy was the hero, with two doubles and a home run. By Game Four, the A's were through. Rudolph baffled them again and scored the deciding run in a 3-1 win that gave Boston its biggest miracle of all: a World Series sweep.

Braves 4
Best Players: Dick Rudolph
(2-0, 0.50 ERA);
Hank Gowdy
(.545 BA, 5 XBH)
Athletics 0
Best Player: Eddie Plank (1.00 ERA)

1915
Philadelphia Phillies (NL) vs. Boston Red Sox (AL)

Fans in the baseball-crazy cities of Boston and Philadelphia were treated to a second straight World Series, only this time it was the Red Sox and Phillies locking horns. Rube Foster, Ernie Shore, Dutch Leonard, and Babe Ruth anchored Boston's starting staff, and the marvelous outfield of Tris Speaker, Harry Hooper, and Duffy Lewis was still intact. The Phillies won games with tight defense and stingy pitching. The star of the team was Grover Cleveland Alexander,

Braves should never be underestimated by a powerhouse club like the Philadelphia A's. The A's hitters fully expected to knock Rudolph out of the box in the opener, but he hit his spots and used his curve to strike out eight in a 7-1 win. Catcher Hank Gowdy, a .243 hitter, battered Bender and reliever Weldon Wyckoff for a single, a double, and a triple. Plank muffled the Boston bats the following afternoon, but as the sun was setting, Philly centerfielder Amos Strunk lost a ball that went for a double. Then Les Mann hit a flair over Collins's head and into rightfield for an RBI single, which was all the Braves needed to win 1-0. James had a little extra whose fantastic sinkerball had produced 31 wins, 12 shutouts, 241 strikeouts, and a league-leading 1.22 ERA. Alex the Great was backed up by Erskine Mayer and Eppa Rixey, both of whom had ERAs under 2.50. The Philadelphia offense was led by Gavvy Cravath—the premier home-run hitter of the Dead Ball Era—and Fred Luderus, the lineup's lone left-handed power threat.

As expected, the Phillies won the opener 3-1 on Alexander's strong pitching. Foster outdueled Mayer to even the series in Game Two, with Boston taking a 2-1 thriller on a single by Foster in the ninth inning. Two days later, the teams reconvened in Boston for yet another nail-biter. This time Leonard held the Phillies to three hits and one run, while Alexander gave up two runs, including the game winner, when Lewis singled home Hooper with two out in the bottom of the ninth.

Even in this pitching-rich era, not even the most spoiled fan could expect the classic World Series mound battles to continue—but somehow they did. Surprise starter George Chalmers limited the Red Sox to just two runs, but Shore was a run better. And once again Lewis knocked in the deciding run. Game Five, back in Philadelphia, featured another fight to the finish. Mayer and Rixey pitched in place of Alexander, whose arm was too sore for him to start. Foster was on the hill for the Red Sox, who went into the eighth inning trailing 4-2. Lewis came through yet again, tying the game with a two-run homer. In the ninth, Hooper homered to dead center to give Boston a 5-4 victory and the world championship. Incredibly, it was Hooper's second four-bagger of the game—the same number he had hit for the Red Sox all season!

Red Sox 4
Best Players: Duffy Lewis
(.444 BA, 2 GW RBIs);
Rube Foster
(2-0, 2.00 ERA)
Phillies 1
Best Player: Fred Luderus
(.438 BA, 6 RBIs)

1916
Brooklyn Robins (NL) vs. Boston Red Sox (AL)

The Red Sox were surprise repeat winners in the AL after owner Joe Lannin traded superstar Tris Speaker to Cleveland. Boston had enough hitting to make up for the loss, and twenty-one-year-old Babe Ruth became the best lefty in the league, with a team-high 23 wins. Brooklyn got to the World Series when the Phillies and Braves eliminated each other in season-ending doubleheaders. Jeff Pfeffer led an experienced pitching staff, while the Robins' offense was powered by a trio of left-handed hitters—Zack Wheat, Jake Daubert, and Casey Stengel. Boston had all the matchups going in its favor and thus was a significant favorite as the series opened at Fenway Park.

Brooklyn manager Wilbert Robinson made a questionable decision by placing Pfeffer in the bullpen and loading his rotation with left-handers to neutralize Boston hitting stars Dick Hoblitzell, Larry Gardner, and Harry Hooper. In Game One, southpaw Rube Marquard took the mound for the Robins against Ernie Shore. Both starters tired late in the game, but the Red Sox won 6-5, scoring the deciding run on a wild throw to third from rightfielder Stengel.

Game Two ranks among history's greatest postseason pitching duels, with Ruth and Sherry Smith tangling for 14 incredible innings. Smith lost 2-1 on a walk to Hoblitzell and a pinch-hit double by Del Gainer.

Brooklyn bounced back the next afternoon, when the series moved to Ebbets Field. Jack Coombs outpitched submarine-baller Carl Mays, and Pfeffer earned the save. Shortstop Ivy Olson tripled in the deciding runs in the fifth inning for a 4-3 victory. Robinson tabbed Marquard to start Game Four, and he was hit hard again, giving up a three-run inside-the-park home run to Gardner in a 6-2 loss. In what was to be the final game of the series, Boston took an early 3-1 lead on a bad hop and a bungled double play, and Shore limited the Robins to three hits the rest of the way for a 4-1 win. Brooklyn fans were left scratching their heads. Their team had scored first in all but one game, yet had just one win to show for it.

> **Red Sox 4**
> Best Players: Ernie Shore
> (2-0, 1.53 ERA);
> Harry Hooper
> (6 R, 2 outfield assists)
> **Robins 1**
> Best Player: Jack Coombs
> (Game 3 W)

1917
New York Giants (NL) vs. Chicago White Sox (AL)

John McGraw returned to the World Series for the fifth time with the same formula that had worked so well in the past—defense, speed, and pitching. After losing the 1913 series, McGraw had dismantled his club and rebuilt it into a pennant-winner in just four seasons. This group, however, did not feature many big-name stars. Ex-Cub Heinie Zimmerman led the NL with 102 RBIs, while outfielder Dave Robertson hit a league-high 12 home runs. New York also got big years from George Burns and former Federal League star Benny Kauff. The pitching staff was led by 21-game winner Ferdie Schupp, along with veterans Slim Sallee and Rube Benton. The Chicago White Sox were chock full of high-profile players. Eddie Collins and Joe Jackson were two of the best hitters ever. Hap Felsch was the game's top centerfielder behind Tris Speaker and Ty Cobb. Young Ray Schalk was a take-charge leader behind the plate, and he handled a staff that included the AL's top winner, Ed Cicotte, and Red Faber, whose spitball reminded some of old-time Chicago hurler Ed Walsh. The Sox were big favorites, and it was not difficult to see why.

Cicotte and Sallee dueled in a marvelous opener, which was decided on a home run by Felsch. The 2-1 win featured a diving grab by Jackson in the seventh and a bullet throw by Schalk to nail a would-be base stealer in the eighth. Game Two saw both teams score twice in the second before the White Sox torched the New York bullpen for five runs in the fourth inning to win 7-2 behind Faber. Benton came through in front of the home crowd after the series shifted to New York, shutting out the Sox 2-0. A 5-0 shutout by Schupp in Game Four evened the series.

Back to Chicago the two teams went, with the Giants seeming to have regained the momentum. Up 5-2 in the seventh, the Giants' wheels came off in two gruesome

Batters could do little with Red Faber's spitter other than pound it into the dirt. He won three times against the Giants.

innings, during which the White Sox collected seven hits and six runs to win 8-5. Faber threw two innings of hitless relief to pick up the win. The series returned to New York, where Faber took the mound two days later against Benton. A pair of bone-headed fielding plays by Zimmerman in the fourth inning led to three Chicago runs. Faber survived a fielding miscue by outfielder Shano Collins and held the Giants to two runs on six hits, as the White Sox wrapped up the series 4-2.

White Sox 4
Best Players: Red Faber (3 W);
Eddie Collins (.409 BA, 34 errorless chances)
Giants 2
Best Player: Dave Robertson (.500 BA, .636 SA)

1918
Chicago Cubs (NL) vs. Boston Red Sox (AL)

With America now fully committed to the war in Europe, major-league teams lost many of their stars for all or part of the 1918 season. The Red Sox did a great job plugging holes, starting with the one created when player-manager Jack Barry was drafted into the Navy. Fifty-year-old Ed Barrow, a respected baseball executive, took over the team and put together a patchwork club that battled the Indians and the Senators to win the pennant. Barrow's toughest challenge was to replace outfielder Duffy Lewis. He did this by playing his best left-handed pitcher, Babe Ruth, in leftfield on days when he was not pitching and the

Red Sox were facing a right-handed hurler. The Babe responded with 40 extra-base hits in just 317 at bats, and he led the league with 11 home runs. Carl Mays, Sad Sam Jones, and Bullet Joe Bush rounded out a terrific starting staff. The Cubs survived wartime player losses, too, thanks to rookie shortstop Charlie Hollacher—who led the league in hits—and veteran hurlers Hippo Vaughn, Lefty Tyler, and Claude Hendrix, who together won 61 games.

The government ended the baseball season on Labor Day, meaning the World Series would be played in early September for the first time. The opener took place on September 5 in Chicago, but Cubs fans went home unhappy. They had watched their boys fall meekly to Ruth, 1-0. The Cubs bunched a walk, a bunt, a single, and a double for three runs in the second inning of Game Two, and Tyler allowed only a single run for an easy 3-1 win. Game Three saw Mays outpitch Vaughn, who was going on just a day's rest, by a score of 2-1.

The two clubs journeyed to Fenway Park, where Ruth pitched eight strong innings and tripled home a pair of runs to win again, 3-2. With the Cubs on the brink of elimination, Vaughn came back, this time on two days' rest, and tossed a 3-0 shutout to extend the series. Tyler and Mays went at it in Game Six, in a riveting contest that saw Boston score two two-out runs in the third inning on a dropped line drive by right-fielder Max Flack. Mays pitched his team out of a jam in the fourth and held the Cubs to only one run thanks to a pick-off, a runner caught stealing, and two wonderful defensive plays. The 2-1 win gave Boston its fifth championship of the still-young century. Amazingly, they would not win another during the 1900s.

> **Red Sox 4**
> Best Players: Babe Ruth
> (2-0, .600 SA);
> Carl Mays (2-0, 1.00 ERA)
> **Cubs 2**
> Best Player: Lefty Tyler
> (1-1, 1.17 ERA)

1919
Cincinnati Reds (NL) vs. Chicago White Sox (AL)

After losing several key stars to the war and tumbling into the second division in 1918, the White Sox returned to the top of the AL behind the pitching of Ed Cicotte and Lefty Williams and the hitting of Joe Jackson, Eddie Collins, Buck Weaver, and Happy Felsch. The Chicagoans were heavy favorites over the Cincinnati Reds, despite the fact that the Reds had captured the pennant by nine games. The Reds boasted the NL batting champ in Ed Roush, as well as a strong and balanced everyday lineup. Pitchers Slim Sallee, Hod Eller, and Dutch Ruether combined for 60 wins and just 22 losses. With World War I over and fans hungry for baseball, the World Series was expanded to a best-of-nine format, with the first team to win five games crowned champion.

Game One began curiously as Cicotte, one of baseball's top control pitchers, hit leadoff batter Morrie Rath, who came around to score on a single and sacrifice fly. The Reds tallied five more runs in the fourth inning, as Cicotte gave up five straight hits before being removed from the game by manager Kid Gleason. Cincinnati won 9-1. In Game Two, Williams suffered from an inexplicable bout of wildness, walking three Reds and giving up a long triple to Ruether in the fourth inning of a 4-2 loss. In both games, Chicago catcher Ray Schalk played brilliantly despite being crossed up time and again by Cicotte and Williams. Schalk reported this to Gleason, who passed it along to league officials.

Game Three saw a heroic performance by rookie Dickie Kerr. He shut out the Reds 3-0 on three singles to get Chicago back in the series. Cicotte personally threw away Game Four, making two errors in the fifth inning to allow the only two runs of the day. Game Five also went to Cincinnati, which won 5-0 on a four-run outburst against Williams in the sixth inning. Kerr returned to the mound in Game Six with the White Sox on the brink of elimination. Once again, he pitched well, winning 5-4. Cicotte narrowed Cincinnati's advantage to 4-3

with a complete game 4-1 victory in Game Seven, but Chicago lost the series when the Reds scored four times in the first inning of Game Eight and went on to win 10-5. Cincinnati's amazing upset victory was viewed with suspicion. Professional gamblers had bet millions on the Reds, and the White Sox performed poorly in almost every crucial situation. Had Chicago dumped the World Series? It would take almost a year for that question to be answered.

> **Reds 5**
> Best Players: Hod Eller (2-0, 15 K);
> Dutch Ruether
> (1-0, two 3B, 4 RBIs)
> **White Sox 3**
> Best Player: Dickie Kerr
> (2-0, 1.42 ERA)

CHAPTER 4

THE 1920s

1920
Brooklyn Robins (NL) vs. Cleveland Indians (AL)

The clash between the Indians and Robins began as baseball's darkest chapter was unfolding. In September, eight members of the league-leading Chicago White Sox were implicated in a plot to fix the previous year's World Series. Chicago Owner Charles Comiskey immediately suspended those involved, enabling the Indians to slip into first place. Cleveland's pennant came at a high cost, however. Shortstop Ray Chapman, the city's most popular player, died that summer after being hit in the temple with a pitch by Carl Mays of the Yankees.

The Indians relied on clutch hitting by Larry Gardner, Elmer Smith, and player-manager Tris Speaker, who batted a robust .388 at the age of 32. Their pitching staff featured 31-game winner Jim Bagby, Stan Coveleski, and late-season call-up Duster Mails. The Robins were led by Zach Wheat, Hy Meyers, Jeff Pfeffer, Sherry Smith, and Rube Marquard, all holdovers from the 1916 pennant winner. Their new pitching ace was 26-year-old Burleigh Grimes, a spitball specialist with the NL's lowest ERA.

The World Series was a best-of-nine

Jim Bagby of the Indians warms up for Game Five of the 1920 World Series. He hit a homer in the contest and was the beneficiary of a rare unassisted triple play.

format once again, and both teams prepared themselves for the long haul. The Indians started Coveleski, a master of control, in Game One, and he beat Marquard 3-1 in an exciting, tightly played contest. Grimes evened the series with a shutout the next day, defeating Bagby. Game Three featured yet another tense pitching duel, as Brooklyn's Smith, a lefty, limited the mostly left-handed Indians to just three hits in a 2-1 win.

The series moved from Ebbets Field to Cleveland's League Park, where Coveleski pitched another terrific game and beat the Robins 5-1. Game Five was one for the record books, as Bagby and Grimes hooked up again. In the first inning, Elmer Smith of the Indians pulled a ball over the rightfield screen with the bases loaded, for the first grand slam in World Series history. In the fourth, Brooklyn reliever Clarence Mitchell walked catcher Steve O'Neill to get to Bagby, who promptly hammered a ball over the centerfield fence for the first home run by a pitcher in World Series history. An inning later, Cleveland second baseman Bill Wambsganss speared a line drive by Mitchell and pulled off the first unassisted triple play in World Series history. Their spirit broken, the Robins lost 8-1 and went down in the final two games without scoring a single run.

Indians 5
Best Players: **Stan Coveleski**
(3 W, 0.67 ERA);
Steve O'Neill
(.440 OBA, 0.89
staff ERA)
Robins 2
Best Player: **Sherry Smith**
(0.53 ERA in 2 starts)

1921
New York Giants (NL) vs. New York Yankees (AL)

John McGraw was back in the World Series after five consecutive defeats. Win or lose the world championship, however, he had already lost the battle for New York to the Yankees, who were tenants in his Polo Grounds. Babe Ruth had captured the city's imagination and had already begun to change the way baseball was both watched and played. Swinging from the heels, the Babe put up numbers in 1921 that still seem impossible. The big left-hander hit 59 home runs, scored 177 runs, collected 171 RBIs, walked 144 times, and hit .378. To the horror of old-timers like McGraw, who still prized "scientific" baseball, Ruth was cheered no matter how foolish he looked. Ruth's co-conspirator in the Yankee offense was a dour and disagreeable leftfielder named Bob Meusel. In 1921, Meusel socked 24 home runs, drove in 135 runs, and struck out even more often than the Babe. The team's pitching staff was led by Carl Mays and Bob Shawkey. It also featured 21-year-old Waite Hoyt, who won 19 games.

As good as the Yankees were, top to bottom, the Giants still had the better team. Their everyday lineup included future Hall of Famers George Kelly, Dave Bancroft, Frankie Frisch, and Ross Youngs. George Burns was still around, drawing walks and scoring runs from the leadoff spot, and Irish Meusel (Bob's brother) proved a valuable midseason pickup from the Phillies. And a veteran pitching staff was led by Art Nehf, Jesse Barnes, Phil Douglas, and Fred Toney.

Mays opened the best-of-nine series

with a five-hit 3-0 shutout, with Frisch collecting four of those hits. Hoyt followed with a shutout of his own, a two-hit gem that ended 3-0. The Giants came right back in Game Three, 13-5, with Youngs smashing a double and a triple in an eight-run seventh. Douglas pitched a tough game for the Giants two afternoons later, as McGraw's men beat Mays 4-2. Young Hoyt got his second win of the series in Game Five, 3-1, with Ruth scoring the winning run after surprising everyone and bunting his way on base. The Yankees were not only up 3 games to 2, but they were also beating the Giants at their own game.

The rest of the series featured three exciting contests. The Yankees seemed to be on the verge of winning each game, but the Giants took all three. The difference may have been the NL champs' experience, but the absence of Ruth—who had come down with an infected arm—had something to do with it, too. Game Six saw Shawkey blow a 5-3 lead and lose 8-5. Game Seven went to the Giants 2-1, as Mays was victimized by some shaky fielding. Game Eight featured another brilliant performance by Hoyt, who lost 1-0 on an unearned run. The Yankees—so certain they had the series sewn up—never knew what hit them.

Giants 5
  Best Players: Phil Douglas
                   (2 W, 2.07 ERA);
                   Irish Meusel
                   (.586 SA, 7 RBIs)
Yankees 3
  Best Player: Waite Hoyt
                   (0 ER in 27 IP)

1922
New York Giants (NL) vs. New York Yankees (AL)

Never before had a team undergone so much change as the Yankees and still managed a return visit to the World Series. Gone were Roger Peckinpaugh, Chick Fewster, Elmer Miller, Rip Collins, and Jack Quinn—replaced by Joe Dugan, Whitey Witt, Everett Scott, Bullet Joe Bush, and Sad Sam Jones. Home Run Baker remained a Yankee but played sparingly because of injuries. The St. Louis Browns nearly caught New York but came up a game short.

The Giants swapped George Burns to the Reds for veteran third baseman Heinie Groh, enabling Frankie Frisch to move to second base. They also picked up starters Jack Scott and Hugh McQuillan in late-season deals to bolster an underrated pitching staff. The Giants led the pennant race from the opening bell and finished seven games up on the Reds. The winning team in this series would need just four victories, as the three-year experiment with a best-of-nine format was abandoned in favor of the old best-of-seven.

Once again, the entire series was played at the Polo Grounds. The Yankees grabbed the lead in the opener, scoring a run off Art Nehf on a Babe Ruth single and adding another on a sacrifice fly. Down 2-0 in the eighth, the Giants came roaring back. Four straight singles and a long fly produced three runs, which was enough for the win. Game Two was called by the umpires with the score knotted at 3-3 in the tenth inning, and a near-riot ensued. The game went into the books as a tie. Scott pitched a brilliant game for the Giants the next day, winning 3-0.

In Game Four, the Yankees took over as the "home" team, and it seemed as if their fortunes might change when they scored twice in the opening frame. Then the Giants touched submarine-baller Carl Mays for four runs in the fifth, and McQuillan allowed the Yankees just one more run to squeak out a 4-3 victory. The Giants held Ruth hitless for a third straight game and staged an eighth-inning rally to win 5-3. John McGraw had a satisfying sweep, but only because the Yankee pitchers had failed to hold leads in three of the four losses.

> **Giants 4**
> Best Players: Irish Meusel (7 RBIs);
> Heinie Groh (.474 BA)
>
> **Yankees 0**
> Best Player: Aaron Ward
> (2 HR, .615 SA)
>
> **1 Tie**

1923
New York Giants (NL) vs. New York Yankees (AL)

For John McGraw, the only thing worse than having Babe Ruth and the Yankees as tenants in his beloved Polo Grounds was watching them draw crowds of 50,000 and more at the newly constructed Yankee Stadium just across the Harlem River. Nothing short of humiliating the AL champs—as the Giants had in 1921 and 1922—would do. The only significant change in the Yankees' lineup was the addition of veteran starter Herb Pennock, purchased from the cash-hungry Boston Red Sox. Pennock did not throw hard, but he knew the weakness of every batter in the league and could pitch to those weaknesses

with great effectiveness. Ruth, who had rebounded from an off-year to hit 41 homers and post a career-high .393 average, powered the offense, while Sad Sam Jones led the pitching staff with 21 wins.

The Giants were largely unchanged, too. Their everyday lineup featured four .300 hitters, including Frankie Frisch and Ross Youngs, while Casey Stengel turned in his second straight big year as part of a rightfield platoon. The Giants' staff was led again by Art Nehf and Rosy Ryan, with the notable addition of Jack Bentley, who had won 41 games and hit .349 for the minor league Orioles in 1922.

The opener featured a pitching duel between Ryan and Joe Bush, and the game was tied 4-4 into the ninth. In the top of the inning, Stengel hammered a ball to the deepest part of Yankee Stadium and began to run.

Frankie Frisch takes his cuts in batting practice. He rapped out 10 hits in a losing cause against the Yankees.

Somewhere near second base he lost his shoe, but he kept going until he slid safely home with the winning run. Pennock scattered nine hits and Ruth belted a pair of bases-empty home runs in Game Two for a 3-2 victory, but Nehf came back the next afternoon to shut down the Yankees 1-0.

Game Four was crucial for the Yankees, and they played that way, scoring six times in the second inning on their way to giving Bob Shawkey an 8-4 win. The Yankees continued to kill the Giants' pitching in Game Five, scoring seven runs in the first two innings off Bentley. Bush won 8-1, and the Yanks grabbed a 3-2 series lead. McGraw sent Nehf to the mound in an attempt to stall the Yankee attack. Nehf was excellent for seven innings, but he lost a 4-1 lead and left the game in the eighth with the bases loaded. Ryan came in and let four runners score, and the Yankees went on to wrap up the series with a 6-4 win.

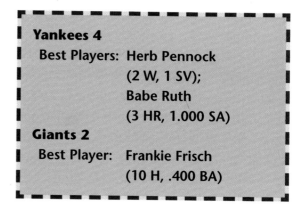

Yankees 4
  Best Players: Herb Pennock
  (2 W, 1 SV);
  Babe Ruth
  (3 HR, 1.000 SA)
Giants 2
  Best Player: Frankie Frisch
  (10 H, .400 BA)

1924
New York Giants (NL) vs. Washington Senators (AL)

The American League leader in wins, strikeouts, shutouts, and ERA in 1924 was the great Walter Johnson. There was nothing surprising about this record—between 1910 and 1924, he had led the AL in these categories a total of 30 times. What was unusual about this season was that the 36-year-old

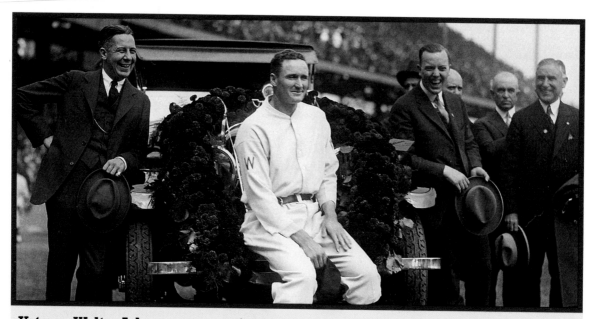

Veteran Walter Johnson poses prior to Game One with a gift from Washington fans—a new car.

was pitching in a World Series for the first time. His Washington Senators had ambushed the Yankees, with contributions from veterans Sam Rice and Joe Judge and young Goose Goslin, who knocked in a league-best 129 runs. Washington's opponent was John McGraw and his New York Giants, winner of a fourth straight NL pennant. New York lacked an ace pitcher but counted six future Hall of Famers in its lineup.

Johnson struck out 12 in the opener but lost 4-3 in extra innings. The Senators won Game Two by the same score on homers from Goslin and player-manager Bucky Harris. The series moved to New York, where a capacity crowd at the Polo Grounds witnessed another exciting game, which the Giants won 6-4. Harris sent veteran lefty George Mogridge to the mound for Game Four, and Mogridge rewarded his manager with a quality start, as Goslin's three-run homer opened the scoring in a 7-4 Washington win. Johnson got another chance to be a hero in Game Five, but he looked exhausted as he started the eighth inning down 3-2. After misplaying a bunt to load the bases, the "Big Train" allowed two devastating hits—including 18-year-old Fred Lindstrom's fourth of the day—and just like that, the game was out of reach.

The Senators rebounded to tie the series back in Washington, where Tom Zachary outdueled Art Nehf in a 2-1 game. Game Seven saw both managers throw everything they had into the game. The Giants had the edge, leading 3-1 in the eighth. Washington loaded the bases with two out, but Virgil Barnes got Harris to hit a routine grounder to third. As young Lindstrom stooped over to field the ball, however, it hit a pebble and bounced right over his head, and two runners scored. Harris then called Johnson into

the game. He allowed six runners over the next four innings but managed to keep the Giants from scoring. In the bottom of the 12th, errors put runners on first and second for the Senators with one out. Earl McNeely lined a single to left, and catcher Muddy Ruel came in to score the winning run.

> **Senators 4**
> Best Players: Goose Goslin
> (3 HR, 7 RBIs);
> Tom Zachary
> (2-0, 2.04 ERA)
> **Giants 3**
> Best Player: George Kelly (9 H, 7 R)

1925
Pittsburgh Pirates (NL) vs. Washington Senators (AL)

The Senators returned to the World Series thanks to big years from a couple of veteran pitchers—Walter Johnson and Stan Coveleski, who was acquired from the Indians—and an offense powered once again by Sam Rice, Goose Goslin, and player-manager Bucky Harris. The Pirates broke New York's stranglehold on the NL pennant with veteran hurlers of their own—Ray Kremer, Vic Aldridge, and Lee Meadows—but it was Pittsburgh's awesome everyday lineup that enabled manager Bill McKechnie to put 8.5 games between himself and the legendary John McGraw. Outfielders Kiki Cuyler and Max Carey combined for 406 hits, 253 runs, and 87 stolen bases, while sluggers Pie Traynor, Glenn Wright, and Clyde Barnhardt each knocked in more than 100 runs.

Game One belonged to the 37-year-old Johnson, who struck out 10 batters in a crisply played 4-1 win. For Game Two, the players wore black armbands in honor of Christy Mathewson, who had died during the night. Pittsburgh fans' spirits were lifted in the eighth inning when shortstop Roger Peckinpaugh—the AL MVP—muffed a grounder and then Cuyler sliced a ball into the rightfield stands to give the Pirates a 3-2 win. The series moved to Washington, where the game turned on a disputed play. Catcher Earl Smith lined a ball to right-center, and Rice made a leaping grab before tumbling over the low fence into the stands. After some delay, he reappeared with the ball in hand, and Smith was called out. The Pirates argued that Rice must have been aided by a fan—why else would it have taken him so long to produce the baseball? The catch preserved a thrilling 4-3 victory for the Senators. Johnson pitched a 4-0 shutout in Game Four to put the Pirates at a 3-1 disadvantage.

No team had ever come back to win a World Series under these circumstances, but the Pirates were determined to prove that there is a first time for everything. In Game Five, Aldridge outdueled Coveleski for the second time in the series, 6-3. Game Six also went Pittsburgh's way, after Peckinpaugh helped the Pirates tie the game 2-2 with a third-inning error. Pirates second baseman Eddie Moore homered two innings later, and the game ended 3-2.

A day of rain and rest enabled Johnson and Aldridge to go again, but neither man was sharp. The Senators scored four runs to open the game, only to have the Pirates get three in the third inning. Johnson continued to struggle but clung to a 7-6 lead as he faced Pittsburgh in the bottom of the eighth. With two outs the roof caved in, as the Bucs touched him for three doubles.

The winning run was scored moments after Peckinpaugh threw wildly to second base for what should have been the inning's final out. Rice, Harris, and Goslin went down in the ninth to complete an historic comeback for the Pirates.

> **Pirates 4**
> Best Players: Max Carey (.458 BA);
>   Vic Aldridge (2 W)
> **Senators 3**
> Best Player: Joe Harris
>   (3 HR, .440 BA)

1926
St. Louis Cardinals (NL) vs. New York Yankees (AL)

In an era remembered for lusty hitting, great defense is often overlooked. The 1926 Cardinals had both. Player-manager Rogers Hornsby—who was followed in the lineup by sluggers Jim Bottomley and Les Bell—had an off year at the plate, but he guided his team to the pennant on the strength of the little things that win games. The enormous contributions of catcher Bob O'Farrell and shortstop Tommy Thevenow do not show up in the stats, but the so-so pitching staff of Flint Rhem, Willie Sherdel, Jesse Haines, and 39-year-old Grover Cleveland Alexander relied heavily on the quick wits and flashy fielding of these two. The Yankees returned to the World Series after a two-year absence with the same good pitching staff, and with Babe Ruth and Bob Meusel in the heart of the lineup. These two were joined by a pair of dynamite young hitters named Lou Gehrig and Tony Lazzeri, as well as a slap-hitting leadoff man named Earle Combs.

Grover Cleveland Alexander, the surprise hero of the 1926 World Series

The Yankees won the opener 2-1 on a three-hit performance by Herb Pennock. Game Two featured a ten-strikeout masterpiece by Alexander, whose sinker worked just as well in the 1920s as it had in the Dead Ball Era. Game Three, in St. Louis, saw the Cards' other old-timer, Haines, fashion a five-hit shutout and hit a two-run homer to win 4-0. Ruth snapped out of a two-for-ten slump in Game Four and went wild for New York. He hit a ball over the rightfield roof in the first inning, and then cleared the right-centerfield roof in the third. In the sixth inning, the Babe caught one perfectly and sent it to the deepest part of the bleachers in dead centerfield. The Yankees triumphed 10-5, with Waite Hoyt picking up the win. Game Five featured less hitting but was just as exciting. Pennock and Sherdel went the distance in a ten-inning affair won by the Yankees 3-2 on a sacrifice fly by Lazzeri. The Cards glumly packed their bags for Yankee Stadium, where they would need to win twice.

Alexander held the Yankees in check during Game Six, while Hornsby, Bottomley, and Bell knocked in eight runs in a 10-2 victory. Alex the Great celebrated hard that evening, assuming he was done for the series. But when Haines got into a jam in the seventh inning of Game Seven the next day, Hornsby motioned for Alexander to start warming up. Still feeling the effects of his night on the town, he came into the game with two outs, the Cardinals up 3-2, and the bases loaded with Yankees. With the menacing Lazzeri at the plate, Alexander gave up a long drive that just curved foul. He then struck Lazzeri out. Alexander retired the Yanks in order in the eighth inning but walked Ruth with two gone in the ninth. With Meusel batting, the Babe decided to catch St. Louis by surprise and took off for second. O'Farrell gunned the ball to second base, and Ruth was tagged out to end the World Series on one of the most idiotic plays in history.

Yankee teammates Babe Ruth and Lou Gehrig brought amazing power to the World Series during the 1920s. Their fame drew enormous crowds on barn-storming tours during the off-season.

1927
Pittsburgh Pirates (NL) vs. New York Yankees (AL)

The Yankees featured the most powerful lineup anyone had ever seen, with Babe Ruth, Lou Gehrig, Tony Lazzeri, and Bob Meusel combining for 333 extra-base hits and 544 RBIs. Not a single Pirate reached double figures in home runs in 1927, but Pittsburgh's slashing hitters—including infielders Glenn Wright and Pie Traynor and outfielders Paul and Lloyd Waner—knew how to move runners around the bases. The two pitching staffs were both very good, and despite all the gloomy predictions, Pirate fans were confident their men could shut down New York's "Murderer's Row."

Legend has it that the Pirates gave up after watching the Yankees hammer ball after ball into the upper deck at Forbes Field in batting practice prior to Game One. The facts simply do not bear this out. The opener was an epic struggle, as the Yankees opened up a 4-1 lead, not on home runs but on Pirate fielding miscues. The Bucs then chipped away at New York's lead but stranded runners on third in the fifth and eighth innings to come up one run short in a 5-4 defeat. The Yankees also took Game Two by stringing together base hits instead of home runs for a 6-2 win. The first four-bagger of the series did not come until the seventh inning of Game Three, which the New Yorkers already had under control. Ruth clouted a three-run shot to make a 5-0 game 8-0. The big news was left-hander Herb Pennock, who had a perfect game going. The excitement ended in the eighth, when Traynor singled to left and later scored the game's final run.

To their credit, the Pirates never gave up. In Game Four, 22-game winner Carmen Hill gave up a monster home run to Ruth, but Pittsburgh tied the game at 3-3 in the seventh. In the end, the series that was supposed to be decided by home runs instead ended on a wild pitch. Reliever Johnny Miljus struck out Gehrig and Meusel with the bases loaded in the bottom of the ninth but then uncorked his second bad delivery of the inning. This one was disastrous, as Earle Combs came trotting home to give the Yanks a series sweep.

1928
St. Louis Cardinals (NL) vs. New York Yankees (AL)

The St. Louis Cardinals returned to the top of the NL with the same so-so starting rotation that took them to the championship in 1926. Almost everything else, however, was different. Gone were Rogers Hornsby, Les

Bell, Billy Southworth, and Bob O'Farrell. New to the team was the double-play combo of Frankie Frisch and Rabbit Maranville, catcher Jimmie Wilson, and manager Bill McKechnie. The team's star was now Jim Bottomley, who led the league in homers and RBIs.

The Yankees were essentially the same group, with Babe Ruth and Lou Gehrig doing the power hitting and Waite Hoyt, Herb Pennock, and George Pipgras combining for 64 wins. New York did not roll over the rest of the AL, however. The improving Philadelphia A's took advantage of injuries to four key Yankees and actually were in first place on September 7. But the Bronx Bombers overtook Connie Mack's crew to win by 1.5 games.

The series opened with Pennock and leadoff hitter Earle Combs out of action. Ruth and Tony Lazzeri were playing, but not at 100 percent. The Cards came into Yankee Stadium confident. They left in tatters. In Game One, Ruth and Gehrig combined for five hits, and Hoyt pitched a three-hitter to win 4-1. In Game Two, the Yankees beat up their old nemesis Alexander and scored eight times in the first three innings to win 9-3.

The carnage continued in St. Louis as Gehrig blasted a pair of homers in a 7-3 victory. In Game Four, Ruth hit three home runs

BEST SERIES BY A HITTER: BABE RUTH, 1928

There have been many hitters worthy of this distinction, including Ruth's teammate Lou Gehrig, whose performance in the 1928 World Series might have been just as good. What made Ruth's so remarkable, however, was that every pitcher who faced him was given strict orders not to let the "Sultan of Swat" beat them—even if it meant giving him nothing to hit.

Ruth got New York's four-game sweep started in the opener with a first-inning double. Moments later, he scored the Yankees' first run. The "Bambino" doubled again in the fourth, driving a ball over centerfielder Taylor Douthit's head. He scored on Bob Meusel's homer. After taking a called third strike on a 3-2 pitch in the seventh inning, Ruth flicked an outside pitch past shortstop Rabbit Maranville for his third hit of the afternoon. The Yankees won 4-1. Grover Cleveland Alexander, the Cardinals' Game Two starter, wanted no part of the big guy and walked him on four pitches in the first inning the next day. The problem with putting Ruth on base, however, was that Gehrig followed. The "Iron Horse" got a sinker that did not sink and sent it screaming into the rightfield bleachers. Ruth led off the third inning with a solid single to centerfield, then scored the first of four Yankee runs to knock Alexander out of the box. After doubling against reliever Clarence Mitchell in the fourth inning, Ruth struck out looking in the seventh. By then the game was in hand, and New York had a 2-0 series lead.

Ruth singled twice in Game Three and also reached on a fielder's choice in the sixth inning. In a daring play, he scored all the way from second base while the Cards attempted a double play. The ball and Ruth arrived simultaneously, but catcher Jimmie Wilson could not hold on to it, and the Yankees had the winning run. With St. Louis reeling, Ruth stepped up in Game Four and finished off the Cardinals. After grounding into a first-inning double play, the fans jeered him mercilessly. Had they been a little kinder, what followed might not have happened.

Leading off the fourth inning with the Yankees behind 1-0, Ruth got his first home run of the series—a rifle shot over the rightfield pavilion. In the seventh, he hit a second home run to almost the same spot, again tying the game. This one was a classic Ruthian drive, soaring high in the air and hanging an extra second or two before dropping out of sight. When Ruth came to the plate an inning later, the Yankees were ahead 6-2, and most of the fight had been taken out of the rowdy Sportsman's Park crowd. Facing Alexander again, he hammered another long, high drive on top of the pavilion in right. It marked the second time Ruth hit three home runs in a World Series game. The round-trip blast was his tenth hit, which set a new record for a four-game series. Not bad for someone who saw about three good pitches a game!

Babe Ruth crushes a double off Bill Sherdel in Game One of the 1928 World Series. In all, the "Bambino" knocked out six extra-base hits in four games against Cardinal pitching.

to nail down a New York sweep, 7-2. The Cardinals were a very good team that ran into a better team at exactly the wrong time. St. Louis would return to the World Series twice before the Yankees showed up again.

Yankees 4
Best Players: Babe Ruth
(.625 BA, 9 R);
Lou Gehrig
(4 HR, 9 RBIs)
Cardinals 0
Best Player: Rabbit Maranville
(.308 BA)

1929
Chicago Cubs (NL) vs.
Philadelphia Athletics (AL)

For four seasons, the Philadelphia Athletics had come up short in the AL pennant race. In 1929, they came together and formed one of history's best all-around ball clubs. Eagle-eyed Max Bishop set the table for sluggers Mickey Cochrane, Al Simmons, Jimmie Foxx, and Bing Miller, who knocked in a total of 462 runs. A veteran staff led by hard-throwing Lefty Grove and George Earnshaw led the league in strike-outs and ERA. The Cubs were almost as good. Rogers Hornsby, Riggs Stephenson,

A quartet of legendary sluggers exchange pleasantries during the 1929 World Series: (left to right) Rogers Hornsby, Hack Wilson, Al Simmons, and Jimmie Foxx.

and Kiki Cuyler each hit .360 or higher, and Hack Wilson led the majors with 159 RBIs. The starting quartet of Pat Malone, Charlie Root, Guy Bush, and Sheriff Blake was tough and talented.

Connie Mack surprised everyone when he sent Howard Ehmke to the hill in Chicago's Wrigley Field for Game One. The crafty 35-year-old spot starter had been scouting the Cubs and knew all of their weaknesses. He proceeded to strike out a record 13 batters with his dipping, swerving deliveries and won a tight game 3-1. Earnshaw and Grove split duties for the Athletics in Game Two, and for the second day in a row, 13 Cubs went down on strikes. A three-run homer by Foxx opened the scoring, and a two-run shot by Simmons closed it in a 9-3 victory for Philadelphia.

With a 2-0 lead in the series, Mack started Earnshaw against Bush. Earnshaw reached double digits in strikeouts, but a three-run sixth inning by Chicago gave the Cubs a 3-1 win. The Cubs looked to even the series in Game Four, opening up a seemingly secure 8-0 lead. But in the bottom of the seventh, Philadelphia mounted the greatest comeback in World Series history when they tallied ten runs. The key play occurred when Mule Haas lifted a drive to centerfield, where Wilson lost the ball in the sun. By the time he tracked it down, Haas and two teammates had scored. The Cubs bounced back admirably in Game Five, as Malone carried a 2-0 shutout into the ninth. But Haas tied the score with a two-run homer, and Miller doubled home Simmons for a 3-2 win. For the fourth year in a row, the World Series ended on an unexpected and exciting play.

Athletics 4
Best Players: Bing Miller
(GW RBIs in
Games 1 and 5);
Lefty Grove
(2 S, 0.00 ERA,
10 K in 6.3 IP)
Cubs 1
Best Player: Guy Bush
(1-0, 0.82 ERA)

CHAPTER 5

THE 1930s

1930
St. Louis Cardinals (NL) vs. Philadelphia Athletics (AL)

In a year that saw offense soar and rumors of an extra-lively "rabbit ball" run rampant, Connie Mack returned to the postseason with the same cast of characters as in 1929. Al Simmons, Jimmie Foxx, and Mickey Cochrane combined for 83 home runs and 406 RBIs to power the Philadelphia lineup. The Cardinals, on the other hand, lacked a big home-run threat. Each regular hit more than .300 during the season, however, and St. Louis actually scored 1,004 runs—53 more than the mighty A's. The main difference between the two teams was the A's Lefty Grove, who won 28 games and led all of baseball with a 2.54 ERA. Philadelphia's other starting pitchers, George Earnshaw and Rube Walberg, seemed equal to the Cardinal contingent, which included wily old-timers Burleigh Grimes and Jesse Haines, as well as fire-balling Wild Bill Hallahan.

Grove and Grimes both pitched well in the opener, but Philadelphia's five hits—including homers by Cochrane and Simmons—were timed better than St. Louis's

seven, and the A's won the game 5-2. Cochrane homered again in Game Two, and Philadelphia scored five more runs while Earnshaw held the Cardinals to six hits and a single run.

The series moved to St. Louis, where the Cardinals rebounded behind Hallahan, who twirled an impressive 5-0 shutout. Manager Gabby Street called upon Haines to start Game Four against Grove, and the 36-year-old responded by allowing the Athletics just one run. Grove limited St. Louis to a single earned run, too. But a throwing error by second baseman Jimmy Dykes led to a pair of unearned runs, and they proved the difference in a 3-1 Cardinal victory.

Earnshaw pitched seven tough innings in Game Five, then gave way to Grove in the eighth. Meanwhile, Grimes was also pitching shutout baseball. Foxx finally broke the game open with a two-run ninth-inning blast into the leftfield bleachers to give the A's a 2-0 win. Game Six, back in Philadelphia, was a 7-1 blowout. Earnshaw, on just two days' rest, went all the way on a five-hitter. As predicted, the mighty A's had prevailed. But it was the pitchers, not the hitters, who dictated the action, as neither team batted over .200.

BEST BASE RUNNING: PEPPER MARTIN, 1931

No player ever dominated a World Series with his speed and daring as completely as Pepper Martin did in 1931. Although Lefty Grove and the A's won Game One 6-2, all the fans could talk about was Martin, who cracked a pair of singles and a double. The play that brought the crowd to its feet occurred when A's third baseman Jimmy Dykes forgot to call time while arguing a play with an umpire, and Martin lit out for second and stole the base with his trademark belly-flop slide.

In Game Two, Martin's heroics continued. In the second inning, he lined the ball to left and ran full out for second. Outfielder Al Simmons slipped slightly when he spotted Martin and was unable to throw him out. With Jimmie Wilson at the plate and one out, Martin dove into third just ahead of Mickey Cochrane's throw. When Wilson lifted a fly to center, Martin came trotting home with a big grin on his face. In the seventh inning, he singled again and promptly stole second. After moving to third on a groundout, Martin tumbled across the plate on Charlie Gelbert's suicide squeeze bunt with the second run in the Cardinals' 2-0 victory.

Martin continued to torture the great Grove in Game Three with a pair of hits and two key runs in a 5-2 win. The Cardinals lost Game Four on George Earnshaw's two-hitter, but guess which Cardinal got those two hits (and stole another base)? In Game Five, Martin turned his performance up a notch. He beat out a bunt, drilled an RBI single, homered off Hall-of-Famer Waite Hoyt, and

Pepper Martin takes a break from his wild World Series to chat with his wife, Ruby.

knocked in four runs in St. Louis's 5-1 win. After the Cards dropped Game Six, Martin saved them yet again in Game Seven. With two on, two out, and the A's two runs down in the ninth, Max Bishop lined a pitch to shallow center. Martin, charging hard, gloved the ball before it hit the turf and kept running right into the celebration. A couple of months later, Martin—an unknown to most sports fans prior to the World Series—was named Associated Press Athlete of the Year.

> **Athletics 4**
> Best Players: George Earnshaw
> (2 W, 2 ER in 3 games);
> Mickey Cochrane
> (2 HR, 1.73 staff ERA)
> **Cardinals 2**
> Best Player: Charlie Gelbert
> (RBIs in 2 Cardinal W)

1931
St. Louis Cardinals (NL) vs. Philadelphia Athletics (AL)

On the surface, the two teams that met in this rematch of the 1930 World Series were little different from the way they were the year before. The Cardinals had two noteworthy newcomers, however. One was Paul Derringer, a 20-game winner in the International League, who was called up and won 18 for St. Louis. The other was Pepper Martin, who had spent a few games with the Cards in 1928 and 1930. He took over in centerfield after Taylor Douthit was traded to the Reds. In an era of scrappy, never-say-die ballplayers, Martin stood out as a supreme hustler, playing every inning as if it were his last.

After dropping the opener 6-2 to Lefty Grove, the Cardinals evened the series thanks to starter Bill Hallahan's three-hit shutout and Martin's inspired base running. Martin manufactured both Cardinal runs himself, taking daring chances on the base paths in a 2-0 win for the cheering hometown fans. When the series moved to Philadelphia for Game Three, Martin received a big hand from the crowd. He singled in the first and doubled in the fourth, scored twice, and stole two bases on the day, as Burleigh Grimes beat Grove on a two-hitter.

The Athletics battled back, with Earnshaw pitching a two-hitter himself to win Game Four 3-0. Manager Gabby Street moved Martin into the cleanup spot for Game Five, and he responded with three hits and four RBIs in a 5-1 victory. Game Six, back in St. Louis, was won by the A's 8-1 as Grove shut the Cardinals down. Game Seven went down to the final out, as Grimes took a 4-0 lead into the ninth but could not close the door. Two walks and a pair of singles made the score 4-2, and Hallahan came on to get the last out. Max Bishop smacked a sinking line drive to centerfield. With the Philadelphia runners in motion, Martin raced in and saved the day with a clutch catch to end the series.

> **Cardinals 4**
> Best Players: Pepper Martin
> (.500 BA, 5 SB);
> Bill Hallahan (2-0, 1 SV)
> **Athletics 3**
> Best Player: Al Simmons
> (.630 SA, 8 RBIs)

1932
Chicago Cubs (NL) vs. New York Yankees (AL)

Joe McCarthy, who skippered the Cubs to the pennant in 1929, had been fired the following year for failing to repeat. The Yankees grabbed him in 1931, and by 1932 they were back on top in the American League. McCarthy's players shared his thirst for revenge after learning that ex-Yankee Mark Koenig had been voted a half-share of the team's World Series bonus money by the pennant-winning Cubs despite hitting .353 for them down the stretch. The Yankees were still powered by Babe Ruth and Lou Gehrig, but they had added young stars Lefty Gomez, Bill Dickey, and Frank Crosetti—and veterans Red Ruffing and Joe Sewell—since their last pennant. Chicago

Boxing great Jim Corbett meets Lou Gehrig at the 1932 World Series as William Collier looks on.

fired manager Rogers Hornsby on August 2 and handed the job to first baseman Charlie Grimm, who did well with a lineup built around youngsters Billy Herman and Lon Warneke and longtime Cubs Kiki Cuyler, Riggs Stephenson, Guy Bush, and Charlie Root.

The Yankees opened the series at home and gave the Cubs a lesson in timely hitting, winning 12-6 despite only getting eight hits. Game Two saw more clutch batting, as the Yankees bunched ten singles to win 5-2 behind Gomez. The series turned nasty once it moved to Chicago, as the fans at Wrigley Field joined their players in taunting the Yankees. Ruth, a favorite target, gave as well as he got, trading obscenities with hecklers after his first-inning home run put the Yankees out in front 3-0. By the fifth inning, however, the Cubs had tied the score.

As Ruth lumbered to the plate, abuse rained down on him from the stands. Some choice words came from the Cubs' dugout, too. Ruth, smiling all the while, yelled right back. The crowd went crazy as he took two strikes, holding up one finger, then two. Prior to Root's third delivery, Ruth appeared to gesture toward the centerfield bleachers. Moments later, he blasted a long homer to that very part of Wrigley Field, then trotted triumphantly around the bases. While everyone in the park wondered whether the Bambino had just "called" his shot, Gehrig came to the plate and lofted another home run. New York added a final run in the ninth and won 7-5. The Cubs made a game of it the next day, scoring four times in the first inning, but the Yankees scored eight times in the final three innings to sweep the series with a 13-6 victory.

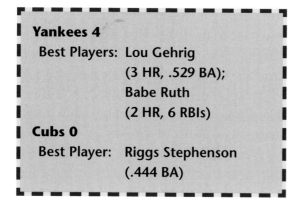

Yankees 4
Best Players: Lou Gehrig
(3 HR, .529 BA);
Babe Ruth
(2 HR, 6 RBIs)
Cubs 0
Best Player: Riggs Stephenson
(.444 BA)

1933
New York Giants (NL) vs. Washington Senators (AL)

A year after John McGraw retired, the team he built during the early 1930s made it past the Cubs to win the NL pennant by five games under player-manager Bill Terry. Terry and Mel Ott made the Giants' offense go, but it was the pitching of Carl Hubbell and Hal Schumacher that boosted the Giants above the rest. In the American League, Connie Mack had sold off his stars to raise cash. The Yankees' pitching never solidified, leaving the door open for the Washington Senators, a team slapped together through off-season deals and managed by its 26-year-old shortstop, Joe Cronin. Cronin, left-fielder Heinie Manush, and first baseman Joe Kuhel led a team of veterans that included 24-game winner General Crowder and 22-game winner Earl Whitehill, who was acquired from the Tigers. The deal that put Washington over the top was getting major contributors Goose Goslin, Fritz Schulte, and Lefty Stewart from the Browns. A lethal top-to-bottom batting order gave Washington a slight edge going into the opener.

In Game One, New York bats made most of the noise. Ott homered in the first inning to give Hubbell a lead that he would never relinquish. "King Carl" struck out ten in a 4-2 victory. Game Two followed a similar pattern, with Schumacher limiting the Senators to five hits while the Giants exploded for six runs in the sixth inning and won 6-1.

It took a 4-0 shutout by Whitehill in Game Three to get Washington back into the series, but the Senators did not stay for long. The next day New York prevailed in an 11-inning battle when Washington loaded the bases with one out but grounded into a game-ending double play. Game Five went into extra innings, too, as the Senators gamely tied the score at 3-3 on a home run by Schulte. The difference was 43-year-old Dolf Luque, who relieved Schumacher in the sixth and went the rest of the way for a 4-3 win.

Giants 4
Best Players: Carl Hubbell
(2-0, 0.00 ERA);
Mel Ott
(.389 BA, 2 HR)
Senators 1
Best Player: Earl Whitehill
(Game 3 shutout)

1934
St. Louis Cardinals (NL) vs. Detroit Tigers (AL)

With the A's dismantled and the Yankees slowing down, the Detroit Tigers were a smart bet to be the AL's "team of the '30s." They had picked up Mickey Cochrane during Connie Mack's fire sale and grabbed lefty slugger Goose Goslin from the pennant-winning Senators to join veteran infielders Charlie Gehringer and Billy Rogell.

Surrounding this experienced core was a group of youngsters all maturing at the same time: right-handed power hitter Hank Greenberg, speedy outfielders Pete Fox and Jo-Jo White, and pitchers Schoolboy Rowe, Eldon Auker, and Tommy Bridges. The Tigers would face a collection of wild-eyed, high-spirited ruffians who knew how to do one thing: win baseball games. Led by Dizzy Dean (30 wins) and his brother Paul (19 wins), the St. Louis Cardinals caught the first-place Giants with a week to go and won the pennant by two games. The hitting stars were Joe Medwick, Ripper Collins, Pepper Martin, and player-manager Frankie Frisch.

The Tigers gave away three early runs on errors in Game One, and Dizzy Dean made them stand up, winning 8-3. Detroit bounced back the next afternoon when Rowe outlasted Bill Hallahan and Bill Walker to win 3-2 on a 12th-inning single by Goslin. The series shifted to St. Louis, where Paul Dean stifled the Tigers en route to a 4-1 victory. Detroit came alive in Game Four, however, racking up ten runs to St. Louis's four, with Greenberg doubling in the winning run. The Tigers also won Game Five, as Bridges defeated Dizzy Dean in a taut 3-1 contest decided by a Gehringer home run.

Detroit fans could be excused for being overconfident. Their team was bringing home a 3 games to 2 lead with Rowe and Auker—each of whom had already beaten the Cards—scheduled to pitch. But Paul Dean was literally one run better than Rowe in Game Six, knocking in the winning tally himself in a 1-0 victory with a single in the seventh inning. Still expecting a World Series win, Tiger fans went ballistic the next day when St. Louis put up seven runs in the third inning. Dizzy Dean, who legged out a single and double in the inning, showed no ill effects of his base-running adventures and limited Detroit to just six hits. Medwick, who had scuffled with third baseman Marv Owen after tripling in the sixth inning, was pelted with garbage when he took his position in leftfield. After a 20-minute delay, Commissioner Kenesaw Mountain Landis suggested that player-manager Cochrane replace him. The game continued, and the Cardinals won 11-0.

> **Cardinals 4**
> Best Players: Dizzy Dean (2 W);
> Paul Dean (2 W)
> **Tigers 3**
> Best Player: Hank Greenberg
> (.571 SA, 7 RBIs)

1935
Chicago Cubs (NL) vs. Detroit Tigers (AL)

The Tigers returned to the Fall Classic with a nearly identical squad, the major difference being 24-year-old Hank Greenberg, who was now the most feared slugger in baseball. Player-manager Mickey Cochrane and second baseman Charlie Gehringer had great years; clutch-hitting Goose Goslin was in his third straight World Series; and the pitching staff was solid again with the quartet of Tommy Bridges, Schoolboy Rowe, Eldon Auker, and General Crowder.

The Cub lineup was different from that of the 1932 pennant winner. Charlie Grimm was now the team's full-time manager, and teenager Phil Cavaretta had taken over at first base. Woody English, Riggs Stephenson,

BEST BROTHERS:
DIZZY AND PAUL DEAN, 1934

The Dean brothers—Dizzy (left) and Paul (right)—flank Tiger ace Schoolboy Rowe prior to Game Two of the 1934 World Series. The Dean boys won four times in five starts.

Seven months prior to the 1934 World Series, Dizzy Dean predicted that he and his brother Paul—an untested rookie—would win 45 games for the St. Louis Cardinals. Dean was off by 4. He won 30 and Paul won 19, for a total of 49. During a wild September pennant drive, the brothers were nearly unbeatable. In a doubleheader against the Dodgers, Dizzy won the first game with a three-hit shutout, then Paul followed with a no-hitter. "I wished I'd of knowed Paul was goin' to pitch a no-hitter," Dizzy kidded reporters. "I'd of pitched one, too!"

and Kiki Cuyler were out, while Stan Hack, Frank DeMaree, and Augie Galan were now everyday players. Chicago's pitching was superb, with holdovers Lon Warneke, Larry French, and Charlie Root joined by young Bill Lee in the starting rotation. The heart of

the Cubs was still Gabby Hartnett, who hit .344 in the cleanup spot during his 14th major-league season.

One out into the opening game, the Cubs had two runs on the board with a double, an error, a sacrifice, and a single.

Against the powerful Tigers in the World Series that October, the brothers did some serious pitching. In Game One, Dizzy got roughed up a bit by Detroit's 3-4-5 hitters (Hall of Famers Charlie Gehringer, Hank Greenberg, and Goose Goslin) but allowed just two hits to the other six batters in an easy 8-3 victory. After St. Louis dropped Game Two, it was Paul's turn to take on the Tigers. Working with two early runs, he shut out Detroit until two were out in the ninth, and Greenberg tripled in a run to make the score 4-1. Paul got Goslin to pop up for the final out.

The next day, Dizzy was asked to pinch-run in the fourth inning. When Pepper Martin grounded to Gehringer, the second baseman flipped the ball to shortstop Billy Rogell with the idea of starting a double play. Rogell stepped on second and whipped the ball toward first, but Dizzy had forgotten to slide. The ball hit him in the forehead with a sickening crack, and he went down as if he had been shot. A hush fell over the St. Louis crowd as their greatest player was carried off the field on a stretcher. "They X-rayed my head," Dizzy announced when he left the hospital a few hours later, "and they found nothing."

With a knot on his head and a grin on his face, Dizzy took the mound against the Tigers the next day, with the series deadlocked at two games apiece. He threw well, allowing just six hits, but his teammates managed just one run to Detroit's three. Needing to win the last two games in front of a hostile crowd, the Cardinals traveled north to Detroit to finish off the series. Paul got the ball for Game Six and allowed three runs through six innings. His opponent, Schoolboy Rowe, also allowed three runs through six innings. In the top of the seventh, Paul followed a Leo Durocher double with a single to right. Durocher scored, and Paul held the Tigers over the last three innings to force a seventh game.

Now it was Dizzy's chance. He stifled the Detroit attack as he had in the opener, allowing six hits and no runs. The Cardinals, meanwhile, jumped all over the Tigers, scoring seven times in the third inning and twice more in both the sixth and seventh. Dizzy contributed a single and a double to the St. Louis barrage and led one of the wildest clubhouse celebrations on record. The Dean brothers had pitched 44 innings, struck out 28 batters, allowed just 35 hits and seven earned runs, and chalked up each of their team's four wins.

Warneke made them stand up, limiting Detroit to four hits in a 3-0 victory. In Game Two, the Tigers exploded for four runs against Root before he recorded an out, and they went on to win 8-3. The victory was a costly one, however, as Greenberg was hit by mop-up man Fabian Kowalik and broke his wrist.

Game Three went 11 innings before the Tigers scored an unearned run to win. Detroit triumphed the next day on a pair of sixth-inning errors by the Cubs. Down 3 games to 1, the Cubs left Wrigley Field with a 3-1 win behind Warneke in Game Five. The series ended the next day in Detroit. With the score knotted in the ninth, Hack led off with a triple, but Bridges wriggled out of the jam. In the bottom of the inning, Cochrane hit a shot that second baseman Billy Herman failed to handle, and Goslin singled one out later to bring Cochrane in for the win. For the third time in four losses, the inability to catch the ball had cost Chicago a game.

Tigers 4
Best Players: Tommy Bridges
(2-0, 2 CG);
Goose Goslin
(.411 OBA,
series-winning H)
Cubs 2
Best Player: Lon Warneke
(2-0, 0.54 ERA)

Goose Goslin and Tommy Bridges lay one on player-manager Mickey Cochrane, who hustled home with the deciding run of the 1935 World Series.

1936
New York Giants (NL) vs. New York Yankees (AL)

For the first time ever, the Yankees made the World Series without Babe Ruth, who had been released from his contract after the 1934 season. The heart of the great 1932 team was still intact, however, with Lou Gehrig, Tony Lazzeri, and Bill Dickey combining for 85 homers and 368 RBIs, and Lefty Gomez and Red Ruffing leading a deep pitching staff. The Yankee outfield was completely new, with Jake Powell and George Selkirk flanking rookie Joe DiMaggio. The Giants were still powered by slugger Mel Ott and screwball specialist Carl Hubbell, but player-manager Bill Terry was slowed by a bad knee, and his staff was only average past Hubbell. A Yankee slaughter was predicted.

The Giants surprised the Yankees in the opener, with Hubbell taking a 6-1 decision (his 17th win in a row!). Order was restored two days later, when the Yankees' offense exploded to take Game Two. Lazzeri and Dickey knocked in ten runs in the 18-4 victory. Game Three offered fans a pitching duel, which was won by the Yankees 2-1 on an infield single in the eighth inning. The Yanks took a commanding lead in the series when Gehrig belted a home run off Hubbell to spark a 5-2 win in Game Four.

The Giants went down two days later, but they went down swinging. In Game Five, they knocked Ruffing around early and went on to win 5-4 in 10 innings. In Game Six, they got two quick runs off Gomez, but he soon settled down and the Yankee bats did the rest, with 17 hits in a 13-5 victory.

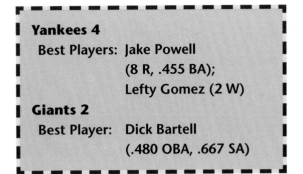

Yankees 4
Best Players: Jake Powell
(8 R, .455 BA);
Lefty Gomez (2 W)
Giants 2
Best Player: Dick Bartell
(.480 OBA, .667 SA)

1937
New York Giants (NL) vs. New York Yankees (AL)

The 1937 Yankees had stockpiled so much talent that their top farm team, the Newark Bears, probably could have finished ahead of half the teams in the AL. Lou Gehrig was still the league's most feared cleanup hitter, and young Joe DiMaggio had blossomed into the finest all-around outfielder in the game. Beyond 20-game winners Lefty Gomez and Red Ruffing, manager Joe McCarthy could start any of five effective pitchers.

The Giants, on the other hand, had just enough to squeak past the Cubs in a late-season series and win the pennant by three games. Bill Terry had become the full-time manager, and Mel Ott became a part-time third baseman when Terry could find no one to do the job. Shortstop Dick Bartell steadied the infield and got things going on offense from the number-two spot. Rookie Cliff "Mickey Mouse" Melton came out of nowhere to win 20 games. Every day it seemed someone else came through with a clutch hit or a big catch, which is how you win pennants. Of course, it did not hurt to have Carl Hubbell pitching every fourth day.

Things started badly for the Giants

Joe DiMaggio laces a single off Carl Hubbell in the opening frame of the 1937 World Series.

when the Yankee hitters solved Hubbell's screwball in Game One and put up seven runs in the sixth inning for an 8-1 victory. Things went from bad to worse in Game Two, when Melton squandered an early lead and the Giants' bullpen could not stop the bleeding. When it was over, Ruffing had an 8-1 win.

The series moved across the river to the Polo Grounds, where Monte Pearson baffled the Giants and won 5-1. Finally, in the fourth game, the Giants broke through, scoring six times off Bump Hadley in the second inning. Hubbell was fantastic, going the distance for a 7-3 victory. What little hope was left in the stands at the Polo

Grounds disappeared the following day in the fifth inning. With the score tied 2-2, Tony Lazzeri tripled, Gomez singled, and Gehrig doubled to make it 4-2. That is how it ended, as Gomez snuffed out rallies in the sixth, seventh, and eighth innings.

Yankees 4
Best Players: Lefty Gomez
(2-0, 1.50 ERA);
George Selkirk
(5 R, 6 RBIs)
Giants 1
Best Player: Jo-Jo Moore (.391 BA)

1938
Chicago Cubs (NL) vs. New York Yankees (AL)

After finishing second to the Giants two years in a row, the Cubs prevailed in an exciting four-team race. The season was decided by player-manager Gabby Hartnett's famous ninth-inning twilight homer against the Pirates in the pennant-clinching series. The 37-year-old catcher assumed managing duties after the All-Star break and led the team to 21 wins in its final 25 games. Bill Lee was now the team's ace, and young Clay Bryant stepped into the rotation and won 19 games. Beyond these two, however, the pitching was very thin. The team's best hurler down the stretch was actually sore-armed Dizzy Dean, who was reduced to changing speed and nibbling with his curveball. The Chicago offense was good at every position but not great at any one. The Yankees, who ran away with the AL pennant again, worked 23-year-olds Joe Gordon and Tommy Henrich into the lineup and, once more, got an excellent year from starting pitchers Lefty Gomez and Red Ruffing. The Cubs, it seemed, were destined to suffer the same fate as the Giants the year before.

The wind was blowing in at Wrigley Field in the opener, and the Yankee lineup was robbed of its awesome power. But the New Yorkers knew how to adjust, and adjust they did against Lee. Smart hitting and heads-up base running accounted for two runs in the second inning, and Henrich scored the final run on a Bill Dickey single in the sixth for a 3-1 win. Dean befuddled the Yankees in Game Two and carried a 3-2 lead into the eighth inning. Today, a manager would pat him on the rear and hand the ball to a setup man or a "closer." But in 1938, there was no such thing. An exhausted Dean gave up two-run homers to Frank Crosetti and Joe DiMaggio to lose 6-3.

The Yankees looked to close things out at home in New York. Monte Pearson got them halfway there with a beautiful 5-2 complete-game victory in Game Three. This time it was Gordon who brought home the deciding run. Game Four matched Lee against Ruffing again, and for the second time Ruffing emerged victorious. Hits by Ruffing and Crosetti produced three runs in the second inning, and Henrich put the game away with a solo home run in the sixth. Everyone knew the Yankees were one of the all-time great teams, but now it was in the record books: for the first time in history, there was a consecutive three-time world champion.

Yankees 4
Best Players: Red Ruffing (2-0); Joe Gordon (.400 BA, 6 RBIs)
Cubs 0
Best Player: Joe Marty (.500 BA, 5 RBIs)

1939
Cincinnati Reds (NL) vs. New York Yankees (AL)

The Yankees, winners of 106 games, reached the World Series for the fourth consecutive season. They did so without the great Lou Gehrig, whose crippling disease had limited him to a captain's role on the bench. Twenty-two-year-old Charlie Keller blasted his way into the starting lineup with a .334 average, enabling Joe McCarthy to bat him third and drop Joe DiMaggio into the cleanup spot vacated by Gehrig. Red Ruffing, Lefty Gomez, and reliever Johnny Murphy once again led the staff, though Gomez ended the year with a sore arm.

The Cincinnati Reds made it to the World Series on the arms of workhorses Paul Derringer and Bucky Walters, who combined for 52 wins. The offense featured RBI machine Frank McCormick, slashing Ival Goodman, and slugging catcher Ernie Lombardi.

At Yankee Stadium, Ruffing and Derringer tangled in a mesmerizing opener that went to the ninth tied 1-1. New York prevailed when Keller hit a booming triple and Bill Dickey singled him home. Game Two also went to the Yankees, as Monte Pearson exhibited unusually good control in a 4-0 shutout. Any hope the Reds had of staging a comeback at Crosley Field disappeared in the fifth inning of Game Three, when Keller blasted his second two-run homer of the game for the final runs in a 7-3 Yankee victory.

Derringer took the mound for the des-perate Reds in Game Four and pitched well. He left for a pinch hitter in the seventh, entrusting a 3-2 lead to Walters. The Reds added a run in the eighth, but Walters could not hold the Yankees, who tied the game in the ninth. It all came apart in the tenth, when DiMaggio singled with men on first and second. Frank Crosetti came in to score, then Keller tried for home when Goodman bobbled the ball in the outfield. Keller collided with Lombardi at the plate, and the ball trickled away. DiMaggio came all the way around and scored, too, giving New York a 7-4 win and a series sweep.

Yankees 4
Best Players: Charlie Keller
(3 HR, 8 R, .438 BA);
Red Ruffing
(4-hit W in opener)
Reds 0
Best Player: Paul Derringer
(2 GS, 2.35 ERA)

CHAPTER 6

THE 1940s

1940
Cincinnati Reds (NL)
vs. Detroit Tigers (AL)

Detroit's season was made in the spring, when manager Del Baker shifted Hank Greenberg to leftfield and installed backup catcher Rudy York as his first baseman. York smashed 34 homers and knocked in 134 runs, while Greenberg led the league with 41 home runs and 150 RBIs. Schoolboy Rowe and Tommy Bridges were still reliable starters for the Tigers, but veteran Bobo Newsom was the team's top winner with 21 victories. Virtually unchanged from 1939, the Reds were led again by the pitching of Paul Derringer and Bucky Walters and the hitting of Frank McCormick and Ernie Lombardi. An ankle injury sidelined Lombardi in September, so the Reds pressed 39-year-old coach Jimmie Wilson into service, and the former Cardinal did a great job.

In Game One, the Tigers torched Derringer in front of his home fans, scoring five times in the second inning to set up a 7-2 victory. Walters had better luck the next day, overcoming some early wildness and limiting the Tigers to three hits in a 5-3 win. The series shifted to Detroit, where the Tigers blew open a 1-1 game in the seventh inning on home runs by York and Pinky Higgins. Bridges scattered ten Cincinnati hits to prevail by a score of 7-4. Needing a win badly, the Reds sent their ace, Derringer, back to the mound for Game Four. He responded with a 5-2 complete-game victory.

In Game Five, Greenberg hammered a three-run homer into the upper deck and added a sacrifice fly to power Detroit's 8-0 victory. Newsom got the shutout for his second win of the series. Back in Cincinnati, the Reds looked to Walters to keep them alive, and he did not disappoint. The crafty right-hander not only hurled a shutout, but also homered to cap off a 4-0 win. Game Seven pitted Newsom against Derringer. The Tigers struck first, scoring a run in the third on Charlie Gehringer's infield hit. The Reds came back in the seventh, when McCormick doubled off the leftfield wall. Jimmy Ripple hit a ball against the screen in right; Bruce Campbell fielded it perfectly and gunned toward home plate. The lumbering McCormick appeared to be a dead duck, but shortstop Dick Bartell—with his back to the play—cut the ball off, hoping to nail Ripple at second. Both runners were safe; the score was tied; and two batters later, Ripple scored the series-winning run on a sacrifice fly.

```
Reds 4
  Best Players:  Bucky Walters
                 (2-0, 1.50 ERA);
                 Paul Derringer
                 (2-1, 2.79 ERA)
Tigers 3
  Best Player:   Bobo Newsom
                 (2-1, 1.38 ERA)
```

1941
Brooklyn Dodgers (NL) vs. New York Yankees (AL)

The summer of 1941 featured a 56-game hitting streak by Joe DiMaggio, a successful assault on the .400 mark by Ted Williams, and a dogfight between the Dodgers and the Cardinals for the NL pennant. Brooklyn, managed by feisty Leo Durocher, had the league's best power hitter in first baseman Dolph Camilli. They also claimed its most exciting player in Pete Reiser, who won the batting crown in his first full season. The Dodger pitching staff featured starters Kirby Higbe and Whit Wyatt and ace reliever Hugh Casey. The Yankees blew away the competition in the AL, with DiMaggio and Charlie Keller's lethal righty-lefty combo in the heart of the order. New to the team was shortstop Phil Rizzuto, who batted .307. Lefty Gomez bounced back from shoulder problems to lead a pitching staff that included left-hander Marius Russo, reliever Johnny Murphy, and 37-year-old Red Ruffing, who was still good for 15 wins.

The series opener marked the first time the Dodgers set foot in gigantic Yankee Stadium. They found it to their liking, winning Game Two 3-2 after dropping Game One by the same score. The Yankees enjoyed their first game at tiny Ebbets Field, scoring twice off of Casey on singles by DiMaggio and Keller for a 2-1 win. Three exciting one-run games had electrified the city's baseball fans, but the best was yet to come.

In Game Four, the Yankees scored three times in the first four innings, but Brooklyn responded with four runs on a pinch-hit double by Jimmy Wasdell and a two-run homer by Reiser. The game went into the ninth with the Dodgers clinging to their one-run lead. Casey, who had come on in the fifth inning and retired Joe Gordon with the bases jammed, had held the Yanks in check through the sixth, seventh, and eighth. The imposing right-hander retired the first two batters on groundouts and got two strikes on Tommy Henrich. Then Casey uncorked a pitch that fooled both Henrich and catcher Mickey Owen. Henrich swung meekly at the dipping delivery (which might have been an illegal spitball). The ball glanced off Owen's glove and rolled to the backstop, allowing the alert Henrich to reach first base. Before Casey recorded another out, DiMaggio singled, Keller doubled, Bill Dickey drew a walk, and Gordon doubled to give the Yanks a miracle 7-4 win. The Dodgers went quietly in Game Five, with Yankees starter Ernie Bonham allowing just one hit after the fourth inning in a 3-1 win.

```
Yankees 4
  Best Players:  Joe Gordon (.500 BA,
                 .667 OBA, .929 SA);
                 Charlie Keller
                 (5 R, 5 RBIs)
Dodgers 1
  Best Player:   Whit Wyatt
                 (1-1, 14 K, 2.50 ERA)
```

1942

St. Louis Cardinals (NL) vs. New York Yankees (AL)

The Cardinals were young and fast and nearly as brash as the great team of the early 1930s. Led by outfielders Enos Slaughter and Stan Musial and pitchers Mort Cooper and Johnny Beazley, St. Louis erased Brooklyn's 10.5-game summertime lead by playing .800 ball down the stretch. Returning to the top of the AL were the Yankees, who boasted three of the league's most feared hitters in Joe Gordon, Joe DiMaggio, and Charlie Keller. With the war heating up and the draft starting to drain major-league rosters, everyone knew that this would be the last "pure" World Series in a while. Who could ask for a better matchup than history's best postseason ball club versus the youngest, most exciting team in baseball?

The Yanks took the opener 7-4 behind 38-year-old Red Ruffing. They looked like they might drop the Cardinals in Game Two when Keller hit a ball over the roof at Sportsman's Park to tie the game 3-3 in the top of the eighth. But Musial singled home Slaughter in the bottom of the eighth, and Slaughter threw out a man at third base in the top of the ninth to help Beazley work out of a jam and even the series.

Game Three saw more great outfield defense. With St. Louis clinging to a 1-0 lead, centerfielder Terry Moore made a diving grab of a DiMaggio line drive, and Musial plucked a Gordon bomb right out of the leftfield seats. Not to be outdone, Slaughter made a leaping catch in rightfield to rob Keller of a sure home run. The awestruck Yankees lost 2-0. Game Four brought more surprises, as St. Louis put six runs on the board and held on to win 9-6. Suddenly the unthinkable seemed possible: the Yankees were in danger of losing three straight at Yankee Stadium. And that is precisely what happened. The two teams traded punches for eight innings in Game Five, entering the ninth tied 2-2. St. Louis third baseman Whitey Kurowski came up against Ruffing with one on and one out and curled a fly ball around the leftfield foul pole for a two-run homer. Beazley got the final three outs, and the Cardinals were the unlikely world champions of the 1942 season.

Cardinals 4
Best Players: Johnny Beazley (2 W);
Enos Slaughter
(2 game-saving
defensive plays)
Yankees 1
Best Player: Spud Chandler
(Game 1 SV,
1 ER in Game 3)

1943

St. Louis Cardinals (NL) vs. New York Yankees (AL)

In a normal season, the Yankees would have been licking their chops at the thought of avenging their shocking loss to the Cardinals in the previous year's World Series. But 1943 was no ordinary year. The war had taken from the New York roster no fewer than six frontline players: Joe DiMaggio, Phil Rizzuto, Buddy Hassett, George Selkirk, Tommy Henrich, and Red Ruffing. The team that took the field against St. Louis featured unknowns like Tuck Stainback, Billy Johnson, Johnny Lindell, Bruce

Wensloff, and Nick Etten. Etten, picked up from the lowly Phillies, led the team with 107 RBIs. The pitching staff was led by Spud Chandler, who blossomed into a 20-game winner at the age of 34.

The Cardinals suffered losses, too, but had enough players in their deep farm system to plug the holes created by the departures of Terry Moore, Enos Slaughter, Howie Pollet, and Johnny Beazley. Mort Cooper topped 20 wins again, and Stan Musial led the league in hits, doubles, triples, batting, and slugging.

St. Louis fans barely batted an eye when their team lost the opener 4-2. The series had started the same way in 1942, but then the Cards had swept the next four. The Redbirds did indeed take the next game, on a two-run homer by Ray Sanders and a six-hitter by Cooper. Game Three, the third in Yankee Stadium, went to the home team, however, as the Yankees pounced on Al Brazle for five runs in the eighth to win 6-2.

In St. Louis, the Yankee bats were quieted. But the Cardinals could not touch Marius Russo, who allowed just one run on seven hits. It was Russo who broke a 1-1 tie in the eighth when he doubled and scored the game's final run to give the Yanks a 3 games to 1 advantage. Game Five was another pitching battle, with Chandler and Cooper working in and out of trouble for nine innings. Chandler scattered ten hits and allowed no runs, and Cooper was almost as good. Then, with two out in the sixth, Cooper served up a ground-ball single to Keller and threw one down the middle to Bill Dickey, who lofted a long, high home run that accounted for the game's only two runs and delivered the championship to the Bronx Bombers.

> **Yankees 4**
> **Best Players:** Spud Chandler
> (2-0, 0.50 ERA);
> Bill Dickey
> (series-winning H,
> 1.46 staff ERA)
> **Cardinals 1**
> **Best Player:** Marty Marion (.714 SA)

1944
St. Louis Cardinals (NL) vs. St. Louis Browns (AL)

How dramatically did World War II siphon off talent from major-league baseball? That question is best answered by the 1944 St. Louis Browns. A collection of castoffs that started the year with nine straight wins, they managed to stay at or near the top of the standings throughout the year. The smirks and smiles disappeared when the Browns beat the Yankees in the season's final four games to take the pennant. The team was built around the pitching of screwball specialist Nels Potter and Jack Kramer, who had failed in four previous attempts with the Browns. Across town, the St. Louis Cardinals rode the hot bat of young Stan Musial, the leadership of catcher Walker Cooper, and the pitching of Cooper's brother, Mort, to 105 victories. The Cards were heavy favorites to take the first all–St. Louis World Series, which was played entirely in Sportsman's Park.

The Browns managed just two hits in the opener, but they made them count. In the fourth inning, outfielder Gene Moore singled to right and first baseman George McQuinn pulled a Cooper pitcher into the stands to give their team a 2-1 win. The underdogs nearly took Game Two, but the Cardinals won 3-2 in 11 innings. The Browns sent Kramer to the mound for Game Three, and he turned in a marvelous performance, striking out ten and allowing just two earned runs. The Browns put the game away early, rallying for four runs after two were out in the third inning. Up 2 games to 1, they needed just two more wins to pull off one of the most amazing upsets in history.

The Cardinal batters finally woke up with a dozen hits in Game Four, and veteran Harry Brecheen pitched a complete game to win 5-1 and knot the series. Cooper followed the next day with a 2-0 shutout to put the Cardinals ahead. Max Lanier and rookie Ted Wilks combined on a three-hitter to put the upstart Browns in their place in Game Six, 3-1. Although no one was surprised by the outcome, St. Louis fans gained a new appreciation for their "other" team. Ironically, had the war not come along in 1942, the club probably would have moved to Los Angeles. The Browns eventually moved to Baltimore in 1954.

Cardinals 4
Best Players: Mort Cooper
(clutch W in Game 5);
Max Lanier (solid starts
in Games 2 and 6)
Browns 2
Best Player: Jack Kramer (no ER in
2 appearances)

Cardinal shortstop Marty Marion holds his ground to retire sliding Mike Kreevich of the Browns. The Cardinals prevailed in six hard-fought games.

1945
Chicago Cubs (NL)
vs. Detroit Tigers (AL)

As World War II ended, a handful of the game's top stars began filtering back into baseball. The Detroit Tigers welcomed back slugger Hank Greenberg in May, and his ninth-inning grand slam on the final day proved the difference in a tight race with the Senators. Detroit also got Virgil Trucks back from the Navy, for a starting rotation of Trucks, veteran Dizzy Trout, and MVP Hal Newhouser, whose bad heart had kept him out of the service. The Cubs had it easier, winning the NL flag by three games over the Cardinals, who had lost Stan Musial, Walker Cooper, and Max Lanier to the military. The Chicago lineup was powered by Phil Cavaretta and Andy Pafko, while the pitching staff featured 36-year-old Claude Passeau, Hank Wyse—who overcame a spine injury to win 22 games—and Hank Borowy, who went 11-2 with a 2.14 ERA after being purchased from the Yankees in late July.

Detroit got off on the wrong foot in the opener when Newhouser was bombed in front of a stunned crowd at Tiger Stadium. Borowy threw nine scoreless innings to give the Cubs a 9-0 win. Greenberg hit a three-run homer the next day to give Trucks and the Tigers a 4-1 victory. Game Three went to the Cubs, as Passeau authored one of the most masterful World Series pitching performances ever. The Tigers managed just one hit and one walk in a 3-0 loss.

Needing three victories at Wrigley Field to win the series, Detroit got started with a 4-1 win by Trout. Another easy win followed, as Newhouser struck out nine in an 8-4 decision over Borowy. The Cubs, suddenly facing elimination, battled hard to contain the Tigers, who scored four runs in the eighth inning to tie Game Six. In came Borowy, who held Detroit hitless over the next four innings. Chicago won 8-7 in the 12th to force a seventh game. Cubs manager Charlie Grimm gambled that Borowy had something left for the finale, but Borowy gave up hits to the first three Tiger batters in the first inning, and Detroit had five runs before the Cubs came to bat. Newhouser struck out ten this time and won 9-3.

Tigers 4
Best Players: Hal Newhouser (2 W);
Hank Greenberg
(.696 SA, 7 RBIs)
Cubs 3
Best Player: Phil Cavaretta
(.423 BA)

Tiger manager Steve O'Neill shakes hands with his two stars, pitcher Hal Newhouser (left) and outfielder Hank Greenberg (right).

1946
St. Louis Cardinals (NL) vs. Boston Red Sox (AL)

The first "full-strength" World Series in four years featured the powerful Red Sox versus the slashing Cardinals. MVP Stan Musial led St. Louis to its fourth pennant in five seasons, but it took a playoff win over the Dodgers to do it. The Cardinals got a big year out of Enos Slaughter, who led the league with 130 RBIs, and swingman Murray Dickson, who appeared in 47 games, winning 15 and losing just 6. Howie Pollet and Harry Brecheen rounded out a good staff.

The Red Sox had the AL MVP in Ted Williams, along with RBI men Rudy York and Bobby Doerr and shortstop Johnny Pesky, who led the league in hits. Boo Ferriss, who fought the Germans (and asthma) during the war, improved upon his surprising 21 wins in 1945 to finish 25-9 in 1946.

The Cardinals lost the opener at home, with York homering for Boston in the tenth inning for a 3-2 win. Game Two went to the crafty Brecheen, who baffled the Red Sox in a 3-0 shutout. The series shifted to Fenway Park, where Boston bounced back with a 4-0 shutout from Ferriss on a three-run homer by York. The Cards knotted things the next afternoon 12-3, on 20 hits. In Game Five, the Red Sox got to Pollet early and then beat up on the St. Louis bullpen for a 6-3 win.

Needing two wins to edge Boston, the Cardinals returned home and sent Brecheen to the mound. Once again, the 31-year-old

responded with a beautifully pitched game and a 4-1 win. Game Seven began as a battle between Ferriss and Dickson, with the Cardinals taking a 3-1 lead into the eighth inning. Dickson faltered, and manager Eddie Dyer called upon Brecheen once again. This time Boston got the better of him, as Dom DiMaggio doubled home two runners to tie the game. Slaughter led off the bottom of the eighth with a single, and two outs later, Harry Walker lashed a pitch to right-centerfield as the speedy Slaughter tried to round the bases. Leon Culberson's relay throw to Pesky was a good one, but Pesky—surprised to see Slaughter steaming for the plate—hesitated for an instant before firing the ball home. Slaughter slid safely, and the Cardinals went up 4-3. Brecheen gave up two hits to lead off the ninth but then managed to work out of the jam for his third win of the series.

Boston's Pinky Higgins takes a throw from pitcher Boo Ferriss, who caught Cardinal star Stan Musial wandering too far off second. The play killed a first-inning threat by St. Louis in Game Three, which the Red Sox won 4-0.

> **Cardinals 4**
> Best Players: Harry Brecheen
> (3 W, 0.45 ERA);
> Harry Walker
> (.524 OBA, winning H)
> **Red Sox 3**
> Best Player: Rudy York
> (2 HR, 6 R, 5 RBIs)

1947
Brooklyn Dodgers (NL) vs. New York Yankees (AL)

The 1947 season ended as it had begun, with the Yankees and Dodgers at each other's throats. The bad blood started that winter, when New York hired away Chuck Dressen, one of manager Leo Durocher's

BEST PINCH HIT:
COOKIE LAVAGETTO, 1947

Cookie Lavagetto is mobbed after breaking up Bill Bevens's no-hitter and winning Game Four for the Dodgers.

There have been many great pinch-hitting performances in the World Series. In 1954, Dusty Rhodes of the Giants tortured the Indians with his clutch hitting. In 1959, Chuck Essegian hit a pair of pinch home runs for the Dodgers. In 1975, Bernie Carbo's three-run blast off the bench in Game Six saved the Red Sox from elimination. In 1988, Kirk Gibson of the Dodgers turned the entire series around with his one-armed, one-legged homer to beat Dennis Eckersley of the A's. Each of these players has a special place in World Series history for delivering in pressure situations.

Yet what situation could be more pressure-packed than coming up cold off the bench, in front of your home fans, with two out in the ninth, when the man on the mound has a no-hitter? That was what Brooklyn's Cookie Lavagetto—a former All-Star relegated to bench duty after losing four years to World War II—faced in Game Four of the 1947 World Series. To make matters worse, the Yankees' Bill Bevens was wild that day. He had already walked ten men, including two that inning. Lavagetto, hitting for Eddie Stanky, was not even sure he would see a strike.

With Eddie Miksis on first, Al Gionfriddo on second, and the Dodgers behind 2-1, the right-handed Lavagetto slashed an opposite-field double against Ebbets Field's tricky rightfield fence. By the time Tommy Henrich played the carom and relayed the ball to the infield, both runners had crossed home plate and Lavagetto was pulling into second.

Only one pinch hitter in World Series history ever had a chance to break up a no-hitter and win a game with two outs in the ninth, and he came through. A pinch hit does not get any better than that.

most trusted lieutenants. The name-calling got so bad that the commissioner had to step in. Hardly unnoticed was Jackie Robinson's shattering of the color barrier— and his Rookie-of-the-Year performance. Playing a strange position (first base), Robinson nonetheless hit .297, scored 125 runs, and topped the league with 29 steals. The Brooklyn pitching staff was led by 21-year-old Ralph Branca, and Hugh Casey was still the stopper out of the bullpen. The Yankees, absent from the series for four years, returned with new manager Bucky Harris and a new pitching rotation, featuring Allie Reynolds, Vic Raschi, Spec Shea, and Bill Bevens. The offense still was centered around Joe DiMaggio and Tommy Henrich.

Branca started Game One in fabulous form, retiring the Yanks in order four straight times. In the fifth inning, however, he ran into trouble as the Yankees pecked away for five runs. Shea and relief specialist Joe Page made these runs stand up in a 5-3 wins. Game Two featured another New York offensive outburst, as four Brooklyn pitchers gave up 15 hits and 10 runs. Reynolds limited the Dodgers to nine hits in a 10-3 victory. The move to Ebbets Field energized the Dodgers, who scored nine times early and then held on for dear life to win 9-8. In Game Four, the Dodgers found themselves on the verge of being no-hit by Bevens, who had walked eight batters going into the bottom of the ninth inning. Bevens retired two and walked two. This set up a confrontation with pinch hitter Cookie Lavagetto, who laced a pitch against the screen in rightfield, ruining the no-hitter and winning the game.

With the momentum now in their favor, the Dodgers looked to take the third game in Brooklyn. But it was not to be. Shea pitched his second strong game and won 2-1 on a DiMaggio homer in the fifth inning. Game Six went to the Dodgers, however, when they scored four runs to erase a 5-4 deficit and went on to win 8-6. The series finale was a dandy, as the Dodgers broke on top 2-0. Bevens relieved Shea and put out the fire, then Page came on to pitch the final five innings. New York took the lead on a Henrich single in the fourth and added single runs in the seventh and eighth to wrap up the championship 5-2.

Yankees 4
Best Players: Spec Shea
(2-0, 2.35 ERA);
Tommy Henrich (key
RBIs in 3 New York W)
Dodgers 3
Best Player: Hugh Casey (2 W, 1 SV)

1948
Boston Braves (NL) vs. Cleveland Indians (AL)

"Spahn and Sain and pray for rain." This summed up the Boston Braves pitching staff during its pennant-winning 1948 season. When they were on their games, Warren Spahn and Johnny Sain were indeed two of the toughest pitchers who ever lived. When Vern Bickford and Bill Voiselle started, anything could (and often did) happen. The rest of the Braves were lunch-bucket ballplayers who did their jobs quietly and efficiently.

The Indians beat the Red Sox in a one-game playoff to win their pennant, and the baseball world was denied its first all-Boston World Series. The Tribe had a bit more offense but also relied on pitching to get it through big games. Cleveland boasted three ace starters—Bob Feller, Gene Bearden, and Bob Lemon—as well as an excellent bullpen. The Indians were big favorites.

A blown call by the second-base umpire led to the only run in the opener, as Sain beat Feller 1-0. The Indians took Game Two 4-1 behind sinker-baller Lemon, who had the Braves beating the ball into the ground all day. Bearden turned in the third straight Grade A performance by a Cleveland starter in Game Three, shutting out the Braves 2-0. It took until the third inning of Game Four for either team to clear the fence. The man who did it, Larry Doby of the Indians, earned the distinction of being the first African-American to homer in a World Series game. Doby's solo shot produced the deciding run in a 2-1 win.

Their backs against the wall, the Braves finally came through with an offensive break-through. Trailing 5-4 in the sixth, Boston tied the game and then exploded for six runs in the seventh for an 11-5 victory. Mop-up duty fell to the legendary Satchel Paige, who became the first African-American to pitch in a World Series game when he took the mound in the seventh. The series moved back to Boston the following day. The Braves put up another good fight, but the championship went to the Indians, 4-3.

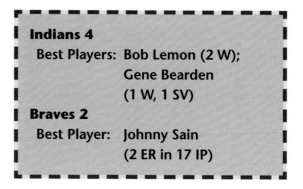

Indians 4
  Best Players: Bob Lemon (2 W);
          Gene Bearden
          (1 W, 1 SV)
Braves 2
  Best Player: Johnny Sain
          (2 ER in 17 IP)

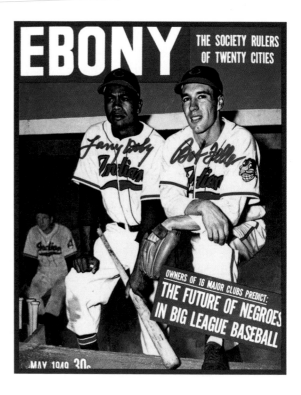

EBONY
THE SOCIETY RULERS OF TWENTY CITIES

OWNERS OF 16 MAJOR CLUBS PREDICT:
THE FUTURE OF NEGROES IN BIG LEAGUE BASEBALL

MAY 1949 30¢

Larry Doby and Bob Feller made the cover of *Ebony* magazine after the 1948 World Series. Doby won Game Four with a home run, while Feller lost a 1-0 thriller in the series opener.

1949
Brooklyn Dodgers (NL)
vs. New York Yankees (AL)

This replay of the thrilling 1947 World Series actually featured better teams. Each had won its pennant by a lone game, so they were razor-sharp to start the series. Each club had also been infused with new talent. The Yankees had assigned key roles to Hank Bauer, Gene Woodling, Jerry Coleman, Tommy Byrne, and Ed Lopat, while prospects Bobby Brown and Yogi Berra had matured into stars. Brooklyn had added Billy Cox, Carl Furillo, Roy Campanella, Don Newcombe, Carl Erskine, and Preacher Roe. The Dodgers had also promoted Duke Snider to the starting lineup and converted backup catcher Gil Hodges into a heavy-hitting first baseman. Jackie Robinson, the

Branch Rickey is surrounded by three stars from his 1949 pennant-winning Brooklyn Dodgers: (left to right) first baseman Gil Hodges, leftfielder Gene Hermanski, and second baseman Jackie Robinson, the first African-American to be named league MVP.

Manager Casey Stengel guided the Yankees to victory in the 1949 World Series. This was the first of five straight world championships for the Bronx Bombers.

league MVP, was now the heart and soul of the Brooklyn team.

The most notable change to either team, however, was New York's new manager, Casey Stengel. Written off as a clown during his days as manager of the Braves and Dodgers, he had seen enough bad baseball to know when he had a good team. And from his years as a player under John McGraw and Wilbert Robinson, he knew how to manage good players.

What many consider to be the best Game One in series history opened this Subway Series, as Newcombe and Allie Reynolds locked horns for nine gut-wrenching innings. Reynolds gave up two hits and fanned nine

Dodgers. Newk struck out 11 Yankees and had given up just four hits when Tommy Henrich led off the bottom of the ninth with a home run into the rightfield stands for a 1-0 win. Roe came back the next day and turned the tables, shutting out the Yankees, with Robinson scoring the game's only run.

Game Three offered fans another tight pitching battle, as Byrne and Ralph Branca traded outs through eight innings, each pitcher giving up just one run. A two-run single by pinch-hitter Johnny Mize and another hit by Coleman made the score 4-1. The Dodgers roared back in the bottom of the ninth with a pair of home runs against Joe Page, but the New York relief specialist got out of the jam with a 4-3 win. The Yankee offense kicked into gear in Game Four,

scoring six runs to Brooklyn's four. The Dodgers' pitching caved in again a day later, giving up five extra-base hits in a 10-6 loss. The Ebbets Field faithful could hardly believe it. After holding the hated Yankees to one run at Yankee Stadium, they got creamed three straight on their home turf!

Yankees 4
Best Players: Bobby Brown
(.917 SA, 5 RBIs);
Allie Reynolds
(1-0, 1 SV)
Dodgers 1
Best Player: Preacher Roe
(Game 2 shutout)

THE 1950s

1950
Philadelphia Phillies (NL) vs. New York Yankees (AL)

The Yankees edged the Red Sox, Indians, and Tigers for a second consecutive AL pennant. Joe DiMaggio finished the year strong; Yogi Berra had a breakthrough season with 124 RBIs; Phil Rizzuto had an MVP year at shortstop; and midseason call-up Whitey Ford energized a 30-something pitching staff by going 9-1.

But the Phillies were the talk of baseball. Young, brash, and talented, the "Whiz Kids" beat out the mighty Dodgers on the final day of the season with a game-saving throw by centerfielder Richie Ashburn and a tenth-inning pinch-hit homer by Dick Sisler. Unfortunately for the Phillies, their pitching staff was a wreck heading into the World Series. Ace Robin Roberts had pitched three times in the season's final five days; Curt Simmons was called in to the Army; and Bubba Church and Bob Miller were injured.

Looking for a little magic, Philadelphia started Jim Konstanty against Vic Raschi in the opener. Konstanty, who had won 16 games and saved 22 pitching out of the bullpen, had not started a game in four seasons. Not to disappoint manager Eddie Sawyer, the NL MVP twirled eight magnificent innings and gave up just one run. Raschi, however, was just a tad better, shutting out the Phillies on two hits. Game Two was another nail-biter, with Allie Reynolds beating Roberts 2-1 on an upper-deck homer by DiMaggio in the top of the tenth inning.

Game Three brought more frustration to Philadelphia fans, as the Whiz Kids blew a late-inning lead on an infield error. With the

New York catcher Yogi Berra tags out Granny Hamner to complete a double play. The Yankees swept the Phillies in four close games.

score knotted 2-2, the Yankees strung together three singles after two were out in the bottom of the ninth for a 3-2 win. In Game Four, the Yankees became the first of the two teams to score more than one run in an inning when they struck for a pair in the first and three in the sixth. Ford got the start for New York and kept the Phillies quiet until the ninth. He lost his chance at a shutout when leftfielder Gene Woodling dropped what should have been the final out of the series. Reynolds came on and struck out Stan Lopata to end one of the most closely contested sweeps in sports history.

Yankees 4
  Best Players: Jerry Coleman
                (2 game-winning RBIs);
                Allie Reynolds
                (1 W, 1 SV)
Phillies 0
  Best Player: Jim Konstanty
                (3 appearances,
                2.40 ERA)

1951
New York Giants (NL) vs. New York Yankees (AL)

After an amazing late-season surge and a pennant-winning home run by Bobby Thomson, the Giants were looking unstoppable as they came into the World Series. Led by Monte Irvin, Al Dark, and rookie Willie Mays, the Giants boasted a solid rotation of Larry Jansen, Sal Maglie, Jim Hearn, and Dave Koslo. They had speed, defense, pitching, and power.

Meanwhile, the Yankees kept rolling along. Clutch-hitting Yogi Berra and rookies Gil McDougald and Mickey Mantle provided spark to the offense, while the familiar trio of Ed Lopat, Vic Raschi, and Allie Reynolds combined for 59 victories. Joe DiMaggio, in the final year of his career, managed just 12 home runs and could not make throws from the outfield. The Bronx Bombers definitely looked like they could be beaten.

Game One, which was held one day after the Giants' dramatic playoff victory over

A trio of former Negro League stars—(left to right) Monte Irvin, Willie Mays, and Hank Thompson—helped the Giants win the 1951 pennant.

Yankee stars (left to right) Yogi Berra, Phil Rizzuto, Vic Raschi, Allie Reynolds, and Ed Lopat head for the centerfield clubhouse at the Polo Grounds after taking Game Four from the Giants.

the Dodgers, found Koslo on the mound against Reynolds. Yankee fans watched in shock as the left-hander shut their team down. The Giants, inspired by Irvin's first-inning steal of home and a three-run homer by Dark, won 5-1. Game Two featured a pitching duel between Lopat and Jansen. Both threw well, but a home run by Yankees first baseman Joe Collins proved the difference in a 2-1 win.

The teams moved across the Harlem River to the Polo Grounds, where Hearn dazzled the Yankees on four hits and Giants first baseman Whitey Lockman hit a three-run homer for a 5-1 win. The Giants' momentum, however, was about to end. Reynolds, who rarely lost twice in a row, hurled a complete game, and DiMaggio belted a two-run homer in a 6-2 victory. After Reynolds's hissing fastball, Lopat's slow stuff put the Giants off stride, and the Yankees prevailed once more, 13-1. Game Six was a tense 1-1 affair until Hank Bauer tripled with the bases loaded. The Giants threatened in the ninth, but Bob Kuzava came on to get the final three outs for a 4-3 win.

Yankees 4
Best Players: Ed Lopat
(2-0, 0.50 ERA);
Joe DiMaggio
(6 H and 5 RBIs
in final 3 W)
Giants 2
Best Player: Monte Irvin (.458 BA)

1952
Brooklyn Dodgers (NL) vs.
New York Yankees (AL)

The Bronx Bombers returned to the Fall Classic for the fourth consecutive year, while the Dodgers came into the series anxious to avenge past losses to the Yankees. Brooklyn featured the same nucleus of Duke Snider, Gil Hodges, Carl Furillo, Jackie Robinson, Pee Wee Reese, and Roy Campanella, but its pitching staff was shaky. The Dodgers did have the "X Factor," however, in Joe Black, a 28-year-old Negro League star who came to the team in May and emerged as the NL's top reliever, going 15-4 with 15 saves.

The Yanks were a solid but unspectacular bunch. Young Mickey Mantle had moved to centerfield after Joe DiMaggio's retirement, and he showed his inexperience by striking out a league-high 111 times. No Yankee hitter had more than 30 homers or 100 RBIs, and only two regulars hit over .300. New York's pitching was aging but still excellent behind hard-throwing Allie Reynolds and Vic Raschi, who combined for 36 victories.

Black won the opener 4-2 with nine innings of six-hit ball, but Raschi came back the next day and pitched the Yankees to a

7-1 win. The series moved to Yankee Stadium, where Yogi Berra's passed ball let in the two deciding runs in a 5-3 win for Brooklyn. In a must-have fourth game, Reynolds came through with a brilliant shutout, striking out ten and outdueling Black in a 2-0 thriller. Game Five went to the Dodgers, as starter Carl Erskine withstood a five-run fifth inning and held the Yankees hitless the rest of the way in an 11-inning nail-biter, 6-5.

Needing a split at home to win their first world championship, the Dodgers sent rookie Billy Loes to the hill for Game Six. The 22-year-old held the Yankees at bay for

The Dodgers celebrate their Game One victory against the hated Yankees. Manager Charlie Dressen is surrounded by (clockwise from upper left) Joe Black, Pee Wee Reese, Jackie Robinson, and Duke Snider.

six innings and carried a 1-0 lead into the seventh. Then Berra and Mantle hit home runs to give the Yankees a lead, and Reynolds relieved Raschi to close out a 3-2 win. In Game Seven, the Dodgers used Black, Roe, and Erskine, while the Yankees countered with Lopat, Reynolds and Raschi. New York was up 4-2 in the seventh when reliever Bob Kuzava pitched out of a one-out, bases-loaded jam by getting Snider and Robinson to pop out. The Dodgers never mounted another threat against Kuzava, who finished the game to dash the hopes of the Ebbets Field faithful.

Yankees 4
Best Players: Allie Reynolds
(shutout in Game 4,
SV in Game 6,
relief W in Game 7);
Mickey Mantle
(winning H in
Games 6 and 7)
Dodgers 3
Best Player: Duke Snider
(4 HR)

1953
Brooklyn Dodgers (NL) vs. New York Yankees (AL)

The cast of characters for the 1953 World Series was identical to that of 1952 with one important exception: Whitey Ford. After two years in the military, Ford had returned to the Yankee mound staff and led the team with 18 victories. Yogi Berra and Mickey Mantle did the big hitting for New York, while Vic Raschi and Ed Lopat backed up Ford in the rotation. Old-timers Allie

Reynolds and Johnny Sain started occasionally but now did their best work out of the bullpen. The Dodgers had one noteworthy newcomer, speedy Junior Gilliam, who took over at second base for Jackie Robinson. Robinson became the team's utility player, manning all four infield positions and also playing leftfield and rightfield. Roy Campanella had a huge year with 142 RBIs, while Duke Snider and Gil Hodges added 120-plus RBIs apiece. The Brooklyn pitching staff featured Carl Erskine, Preacher Roe, and Billy Loes.

Game One opened with a bang, as the Yankees scored four times in the first inning on triples by Hank Bauer and Billy Martin. The Dodgers knotted the game 5-5 in the seventh inning, but Joe Collins homered for the Yanks to break the deadlock, and the Yanks ended up on top of a 9-5 score. The next day found the two teams tied 2-2 in the eighth inning, when Mantle socked a two-run home run to win it 4-2. The Dodgers needed a big performance out of Erskine to get their momentum back, and he delivered. A record 14 Yankees went down on strikes in Game Three, and Campanella homered to give Brooklyn a crucial 3-2 win.

Game Four went to the Dodgers, who knocked Ford out, built up a four-run lead on a Snider home run, and made it stand up, 7-3. The Bronx Bombers earned their nickname in Game Five, blasting four home runs—including a Mantle grand slam—in an 11-7 win. Game Six, in Yankee Stadium, was a classic. Erskine tried to go on two days' rest, and the Yanks jumped on him for three early runs. The Dodgers fought back to tie it in the ninth on a Carl Furillo home run, but New York took their fifth straight World Series in the bottom of the inning on a run-scoring single by Billy Martin.

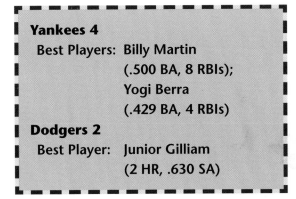

Yankees 4
Best Players: Billy Martin
(.500 BA, 8 RBIs);
Yogi Berra
(.429 BA, 4 RBIs)
Dodgers 2
Best Player: Junior Gilliam
(2 HR, .630 SA)

1954
New York Giants (NL) vs. Cleveland Indians (AL)

It took 111 wins by the Indians, but someone finally figured out a way to keep the Yankees out of the postseason. Everything went right for Cleveland in 1954. The stars starred, and the support players supported them. Hitter Bobby Avila raised his average 55 points and won the batting title. Centerfielder Larry Doby, the AL's first African-American player, led the league in RBIs, and third baseman Al Rosen was one of baseball's best cleanup hitters. The starting staff of Bob Lemon, Early Wynn, Mike Garcia, Bob Feller, and Art Houtteman accounted for 93 wins, while Don Mossi and Ray Narleski formed a dynamite bullpen. Despite winning 97 times, the Giants were given almost no chance. Willie Mays tore up the league and won the MVP award, and rightfielder Don Mueller hit .342, but no one else had a truly standout season. The New York pitching staff, good but not great, was led by youngsters Johnny Antonelli and Ruben Gomez and 37-year-old Sal Maglie.

The Indians got to Maglie immediately, scoring twice when big Vic Wertz tripled off the Polo Grounds' rightfield wall. The Giants scratched out a pair of runs against Lemon to tie it, but the Indians put two men on in the eighth. Left-hander Don Liddle was brought in to face the left-handed Wertz and promptly gave up a 460-foot (140-m) bomb to dead centerfield. Mays, running at the crack of the bat, caught the ball over his shoulder to kill the rally and keep the game tied. In the bottom of the tenth, Dusty Rhodes—a slow-footed pinch hitter who specialized in chipping home runs down the stadium's short rightfield line—came to the plate for Monte Irvin with two runners on base. Lemon delivered, and Rhodes deposited the ball in the stands to win the game.

Rhodes hit for Irvin again in Game Two and singled home a run to tie the score 1-1. The big Texan stayed in the game and gave the Giants an insurance run with a long homer against Wynn in the seventh inning. The series moved to Cleveland with the powerful Indians reeling. The last person they wanted to see was Rhodes, and New York manager Leo Durocher knew it. With the bases jammed in the third, he sent Dusty in to pinch-hit, and he delivered a two-run single that provided the Giants with the deciding runs in a 5-2 win. Durocher did not need Rhodes in Game Four, as the Giants took an early 7-0 lead. Liddle, Antonelli, and Hoyt Wilhelm combined on a six-hitter to win 7-4 and pull off the most remarkable sweep in World Series history.

Giants 4
Best Players: Dusty Rhodes
(6 at bats, 7 RBIs);
Hank Thompson
(6 R, .611 OBA)
Indians 0
Best Player: Vic Wertz (.938 SA)

Willie Mays makes his legendary over-the-shoulder catch of Vic Wertz's mammoth drive. The play killed a Cleveland rally and set the tone for the rest of the 1954 World Series.

1955
Brooklyn Dodgers (NL) vs.
New York Yankees (AL)

Two "old friends" met in the 1955 World Series. The Yankees won a tight three-team race thanks to the power hitting of Mickey Mantle and Yogi Berra, as well as contributions from up-and-coming Elston Howard, Moose Skowron, and Andy Carey. Whitey Ford was joined in the rotation by newcomers Bob Turley and Don Larsen, and veteran Tommy Byrne surprised everyone by going 16-5. The Dodgers were a collection of tough, experienced veterans. Unfortunately, their last five World Series experiences had ended in losses to the Yankees. Their fans were tired of crying, "Wait 'til next year!" Brooklyn won its pennant easily with big years from Duke Snider, Roy Campanella, Gil Hodges, and Pee Wee Reese. The years of wear and tear had begun to catch up with Jackie Robinson, who had moved to third base. Fleet-footed Sandy Amoros was a new face in the outfield, and Don Newcombe had regained the dominance he enjoyed before losing two years to military service.

The first game of the series went to the Yankees 6-5, with Ford getting the win. Quiet Joe Collins, a slugging hero of past

Left-hander Johnny Podres exhibits classic form against the Yankees in Game Seven of the 1955 World Series. His 2-0 shutout brought the Brooklyn Dodgers their first world championship.

ame through with two homers, lded another. Brooklyn fell wo when the Yankees nailed ___s ior four runs in the fourth inning, and Byrne went all the way in a 4-2 victory. Desperate for a win, manager Walt Alston made 22-year-old left-hander Johnny Podres his surprise starter in Game Three. The owner of an unimpressive 9-10 record, Podres went right after the New York hitters and lived to tell about it, winning 6-3.

The Dodgers beat up on Larsen in Game Four, scoring five early runs and hanging on for an 8-5 win. Campanella, Snider, and Hodges each homered in the contest, as Brooklyn pounded out 14 hits and tied the series. Game Five saw Amoros stake pitcher Roger Craig to a two-run lead, and the Dodgers put the game away on an RBI single by Robinson in the bottom of the eighth. Game Six was over after one inning, as Skowron capped a five-run first with an opposite-field home run against Karl Spooner. The Dodgers got just four hits off of Ford, who cruised to an easy 5-1 win. Alston sent young Podres back to the mound for Game

BEST GAME BY A PITCHER: DON LARSEN, 1956

Don Larsen liked to have a good time. He liked to go to parties, stay out past curfew, and drive cars a little too fast. In the spring of 1956, New York Yankees manager Casey Stengel started thinking Larsen was more trouble than he was worth. Stengel almost cut the big right-hander, but then had a sudden change of heart and kept him on the team. He had traded for Larsen after the unpredictable pitcher had gone 3-21 for Baltimore in 1954 to lead the league in losses. Two of Larsen's three victories, however, had come against the Yankees. Stengel was playing one of his famous hunches.

Larsen rewarded Stengel's faith with solid seasons in 1955 and 1956. He was knocked out of the box by the Dodgers in his lone World Series start in 1955, but he got another shot at Brooklyn in Game Two of the 1956 series. Things were looking up after Larsen was staked to a 6-0 lead, but he blew it in the second inning, and the Dodgers went on to win the game and take a 2-0 series lead. New York won the next two contests to tie the series, and Stengel was left with a tough choice: Whom do I start in Game Five?

The manager played a hunch again and went with Larsen. Big Don started well, getting Junior Gilliam and Pee Wee Reese on called third strikes, and then Duke Snider lined out to Hank Bauer in rightfield. Jackie Robinson led off the second inning for the Dodgers, and he hit a scorcher that ticked off third baseman Andy Carey's glove. Somehow, the ball went right to shortstop Gil McDougald, who gunned the speedy Robinson out at first. Larsen continued to set Brooklyn down in

Seven. He scattered eight Yankee hits while Hodges knocked in a pair of runs for the Dodgers in the fourth and sixth innings. In the bottom of the sixth, Alston sent Amoros in to play leftfield. The move saved the Dodgers when Amoros snagged a Yogi Berra fly ball right on the foul line and relayed to first for a double play. Had Berra's hit dropped in, the game would have been tied. Podres settled down and closed out New York 2-0 to give Brooklyn its first world championship in the 20th century.

Dodgers 4
Best Players: Johnny Podres
                 (2-0, Game 7 shutout);
                 Duke Snider
                 (4 HR, .840 SA)

Yankees 3
Best Player: Whitey Ford
                 (2-0, 2.12 ERA)

order, while Dodgers starter Sal Maglie kept the Yankees' hitters at bay. The Yanks got to Maglie in the fourth inning, when Mickey Mantle curled a drive around the rightfield foul pole for a 1-0 lead.

In the fifth inning, Larsen had a couple of scares. Robinson and Gil Hodges hammered pitches deep to the outfield. Robinson's drive settled into Bauer's glove on the warning track, while Hodges pulled a pitch into the gap in left-centerfield. Mantle, racing to his right, gloved the ball on the run. In the New York sixth, Bauer singled home Carey for the team's second run. From there, Larsen was in total control. The Dodgers hit a couple of balls hard but right at New York fielders. Brooklyn's last gasp was pinch hitter Dale Mitchell. He was exactly the kind of batter Larsen dreaded facing. In more than 4,000 career plate appearances, Mitchell struck out only 119 times. On this day, however, Larsen had nothing to fear. Mitchell took strike three on the 87th pitch of the day, and the perfect game went into the books.

Catcher Yogi Berra ran to the mound and leaped joyously into Larsen's arms. The "imperfect man," as one sportswriter called Larsen, had pitched a perfect game.

Don Larsen delivers a third-pitch strikeout to Dodger pinch hitter Dale Mitchell for the final out in the first perfect game in World Series history. Second baseman Billy Martin stands in front of the scoreboard, which tells the game's story.

1956
Brooklyn Dodgers (NL) vs. New York Yankees (AL)

The Dodgers and Yankees returned to the World Series older but wiser. Although both teams were a step slower in 1956, each used its savvy and experience to repeat as pennant winner. Mickey Mantle won the Triple Crown, and Moose Skowron blossomed into a full-fledged power threat. Catcher Yogi Berra continued to produce clutch RBIs and handled a pitching staff that featured Whitey Ford, Johnny Kucks, Don Larsen, swingman Tom Sturdivant, and reliever Tom Morgan. The Dodgers won their league by a mere game, getting a big contribution from Sal Maglie, once their most-hated rival. Picked up on waivers in May, Maglie won 13 games and threw a no-hitter at the height of the pennant race. Don Newcombe was the star of the staff, however, with 27 wins—a total good enough to earn him both the Cy Young and MVP awards. The rest of the squad featured the usual stars: Gil Hodges, Pee Wee Reese, Duke Snider, Carl Furillo, Jackie Robinson, and Roy Campanella.

Their aura of invincibility shattered by the Dodgers' 1955 championship, the Yankees went into Ebbets Field and got kicked around in the first two games. Maglie struck out ten in the opener, with Robinson and Hodges hitting homers off Ford to win 6-3. The Brooklyn offense kept rolling in Game Two, blowing Larsen out of the box in the second inning on the way to a 13-8 win. Up 2-0, the Dodgers hoped to bury the Yanks in their own ballpark. Brooklyn held a 2-1 lead in the sixth inning when 40-year-old Enos Slaughter—picked up as a spare part at the end of the year—belted a three-run homer to boost New York to a 5-3 victory. The Yankees evened the series the next day with a 6-2 win on a complete game by Sturdivant.

The pivotal Game Five found Maglie back on the mound against Larsen. Brooklyn fans were already counting this as a win, but Larsen had other ideas. Inning after inning, he set the Dodgers down 1-2-3. A lucky bounce on an infield grounder and a running catch by Mantle kept the perfect game going, while the Yankees scored single runs on a homer by Mantle and a hit by Bauer. In the bottom of the ninth, Larsen got Furillo to fly to rightfield, then Campanella grounded out to second base. Pinch hitter Dale Mitchell went down looking for the final out of the first (and to this day only) perfect no-hit game in World Series history. The Yanks tried to close it out the next day at Ebbets Field, but Clem Labine outdueled Bob Turley 1-0 to force a seventh game. The deciding contest pitted 22-year-old Johnny Kucks against Newcombe, who had been roughed up by the Yanks in Game Two. To the dismay of 34,000 Brooklyn fans, New York got to Newk again, scoring five times in four innings on a pair of two-run homers by Berra. Skowron capped the scoring with a seventh-inning grand slam, and Kucks was masterful in a 9-0 shutout.

Yankees 4
Best Players: Yogi Berra (.800 SA, 10 RBIs); Don Larsen (perfect game, 0.00 ERA)
Dodgers 3
Best Player: Gil Hodges (.522 SA, 8 RBIs)

1957
Milwaukee Braves (NL)
vs. New York Yankees (AL)

After missing the NL flag by a game in 1956, the Braves rolled to an easy pennant behind sluggers Hank Aaron, Eddie Mathews, Joe Adcock, Wes Covington, and late-season phenom Bob "Hurricane" Hazle. The pitching staff was a good one, with veterans Warren Spahn, Bob Buhl, and Lew Burdette. The Yankees had the same powerhouse of-fense, led by MVP Mickey Mantle and Yogi Berra, along with newcomer Tony Kubek, a superb young utility man. New York's pitch-ing, however, was a mess. Whitey Ford was battling a sore shoulder, which left Casey Stengel to rely too often on second-tier starters Tom Sturdivant, Bobby Shantz, and Don Larsen, who won just ten times in 1957 after his World Series perfect game.

Ford outpitched Spahn in the opener, winning 3-1, but Burdette won Game Two 4-2 on a bloop hit by Covington. The series

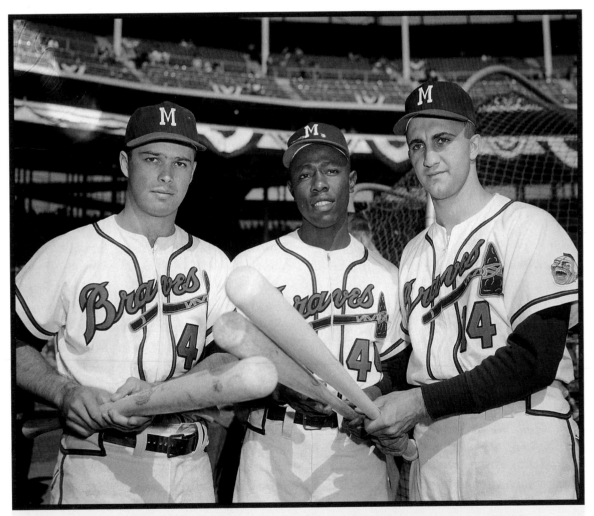

With 6 homers and 14 RBIs, the trio of (left to right) Eddie Mathews, Hank Aaron, and Frank Torre killed Yankee pitching during the 1957 World Series.

moved to Milwaukee, where the fans watched in horror as the Yankees scored 12 runs on 9 hits. The hero in New York's 12-3 victory was Milwaukee native Kubek, who slugged a pair of homers. The Braves averted disaster in Game Four, coming back from a 5-4 tenth-inning deficit to win 7-5 on a home run by Mathews.

Game Five was a tight one. Ford and Burdette traded outs until the sixth, when Milwaukee scored the day's only run on a clutch single by Adcock. The series shifted back to New York, where in the bottom of the seventh Hank Bauer pulled an Ernie Johnson pitch into the leftfield seats to break a 2-2 tie and force a seventh game. The series finale ended in the third inning, when Larsen and Shantz let the Braves score four times. Burdette went the distance for Milwaukee, shutting out the Yankees 5-0.

Braves 4
Best Players: Lew Burdette
(3-0, 0.67 ERA);
Hank Aaron
(.393 BA, 3 HR, 7 RBIs)
Yankees 3
Best Player: Hank Bauer
(2 HR, 6 RBIs)

1958
Milwaukee Braves (NL) vs. New York Yankees (AL)

When the season began, there was little doubt which clubs would meet in the World Series. The 1957 league champions had the best players, and each proved it by cruising to an easy pennant in 1958. The Braves featured the same everyday lineup and bench,

but their pitching staff was without Bob Buhl, whose sore shoulder limited him to just ten starts during the year. The Yankees had a new everyday shortstop, Tony Kubek, with veteran Gil McDougald shifting over to second base. Bob Turley, Whitey Ford, and Don Larsen gave the Yankees a formidable trio of starting pitchers. New York manager Casey Stengel wanted another shot at Lew Burdette, and Fred Haney obliged, announcing that he was prepared to give the 20-game winner three starts once again if the series went to seven games.

Game One was a nail-biter, with lefties Ford and Spahn working their way in and out of trouble. Tied 3-3, the game went into extra innings. Spahn retired the New Yorkers in the top of the tenth, but reliever Ryne Duren allowed three Braves singles in the bottom of the inning and was tagged with the loss. By contrast, Game Two was a blowout after just one inning. The Braves scored seven times, and the hated Burdette delivered the knockout blow himself with a three-run homer. To make matters worse, leftfielder Elston Howard crashed into the fence trying to catch Burdette's ball, and he was lost for several days. Milwaukee won 13-5, and the series headed for Yankee Stadium.

Game Three went to the Yankees, with Don Larsen pitching a beautiful 4-0 game. The Bronx Bombers looked to even things up the next day, but Spahn stymied them again 3-0 on a two-hitter. It was now up to Turley—who had lasted just one out in Game Two—to stave off elimination. To Stengel's relief, Turley completely shut down the Braves, while the Yankee hitters finally beat Burdette by the decisive margin of 7-0. Haney elected to use Spahn in Game Six, and the 37-year-old took the game into extra innings again. Then McDougald hit a homer and Moose Skowron singled in an insurance run, which the Yankees needed to prevail, 4-3.

Burdette and Larsen hooked up for the deciding game of the series, but the Yankee right-hander got into trouble in the third inning and was replaced by Turley. Working his third game in a row, an exhausted "Bullet Bob" used every trick in the book to quiet the Milwaukee bats the rest of the way. Burdette looked just as good until the eighth, when New York finally gained its sweet revenge. A two-out double by Berra opened the floodgates to four runs, and the Yankees cruised to a 6-2 victory. Only one other team had ever recovered from a 3 games to 1 deficit to win a World Series.

Yankees 4
  Best Players: Bob Turley
                 (2 W and 1 SV);
                 Moose Skowron (key
                 RBIs in Games 6 and 7)
Braves 3
  Best Player: Warren Spahn
                 (2 W, 2.20 ERA)

1959
Los Angeles Dodgers (NL) vs. Chicago White Sox (AL)

Casey Stengel had little to worry about during the 1950s, with one exception: Al Lopez. Whether managing the powerful and pitching-rich Indians or the "Go-Go" White Sox, Lopez rarely gave the Yankees much breathing room. In 1959, the White Sox proved that speed, defense, and pitching could make up for the lack of a home run threat when they beat the Indians and Yankees to the top of the American League. The keystone combination of Luis Aparicio and Nellie Fox ate up runs on defense and created them on offense. Chicago's veteran pitching staff was led by Early Wynn and Billy Pierce.

The Dodgers, just two years removed from Ebbets Field, brought a pennant to the L.A. Coliseum after beating the Braves in a season-ending playoff. The Los Angeles lineup featured some old faces—Gil Hodges, Duke Snider, and Junior Gilliam—and some new ones—Charlie Neal, Wally Moon, and Don Demeter. Young Brooklyn holdovers Don Drysdale and Johnny Podres led the pitching staff.

The White Sox defied the experts in Game One with an offensive explosion,

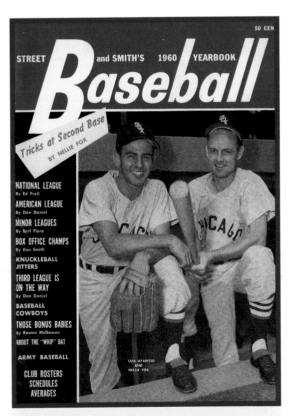

At a time when sluggers reigned supreme, light-hitting Luis Aparicio and Nellie Fox were front-page news.

scoring 11 runs in the first four innings to win 11-0. Wynn twirled seven scoreless innings, and big Ted Kluszewski, a late-season pickup, smashed a pair of home runs. The Dodgers tied the series on two homers by Neal in Game Two, 4-3, with reliever Larry Sherry shutting down Chicago in the final three frames. Sherry repeated his heroics in Game Three, nursing a slim lead for two innings in a 3-1 win. He was also the winner of Game Four, which the Dodgers won 5-4 on a Hodges home run in the eighth.

It was almost a relief for the Chicago hitters to face young Sandy Koufax in Game Five. Although Koufax pitched the game of his life, right-hander Bob Shaw was just a little bit better, and the White Sox won 1-0. Game Six began badly for Chicago, as the Dodgers scored two in the third inning and six more in the fourth. Then Kluszewski belted a three-run homer to grab back the momentum and give the White Sox a fighting chance. On came the nightmarish Sherry, who pitched scoreless baseball the rest of the way to give the West Coast its first of many baseball championships.

Dodgers 4
Best Players: Larry Sherry
(2-0, 2 SV);
Charlie Neal
(10 H, 6 RBIs)
White Sox 2
Best Player: Ted Kluszewski
(3 HR, 10 RBIs)

THE 1960s

1960
Pittsburgh Pirates (NL)
vs. New York Yankees (AL)

The Pirates spent most of the 1950s as the NL's sorriest franchise, but in 1958 they rose from last place to second on the bats and gloves of maturing stars Roberto Clemente, Bill Mazeroski, Dick Groat, Bill Virdon, and Bob Skinner. In 1960, the Pirates led almost the entire way, with help from a pitching staff that featured Vern Law, Bob Friend, Vinegar Bend Mizell, and relief ace Roy Face. The Yankees, looking as if they might repeat their poor showing of 1959, trailed the Chicago White Sox and Baltimore Orioles as the summer commenced. Then the Sox started swinging for the fences and the young Orioles began making young mistakes, and the Yankees ran away with the pennant by winning their final 15 games. New York's power was as awesome as ever, but its pitching was not—not a single hurler managed to log more than 200 innings, and unspectacular Art Ditmar was the staff leader with just 15 wins.

Game One offered baseball fans two surprises. First, New York manager Casey Stengel decided to start Ditmar over All-Star Whitey Ford. Second, the Pirates knocked Ditmar out of the box in the first inning and went on to win 6-2. Game Two featured an offensive show by both teams, with the Yankees collecting 19 hits and scoring 16 runs. Bob Turley let 16 Pirates reach base but allowed only three to score. Ford started and won Game Three with a 10-0 shutout, and suddenly the Bronx Bombers were looking unstoppable.

Law and Face, who combined to win the opener, came back to win Game Four 3-2 and even the series. The next game saw Ditmar get belted around again, and the Pirates won 5-2. The series returned to Pittsburgh, where the Pirates needed just one win to capture their first World Series since the 1920s. As expected, Ford started and pitched another tough game, shutting out the Bucs 12-0.

In Game Seven, almost every move by managers Stengel and Danny Murtaugh backfired. Turley was knocked out after an inning of work, and Law blew a 4-1 lead in the sixth when Yogi Berra's three-run homer put New York up 5-4. The Yanks scored twice more in the top of the eighth, only to see their lead disappear in the bottom of the inning, when the Pirates put up five runs to gain a 9-7 edge. With just three outs separating them from defeat,

BEST PERFORMANCE BY A LOSING PLAYER: MICKEY MANTLE, 1960

A dramatic victory by the Pirates overshadowed Mickey Mantle's wonderful performance in the 1960 World Series.

One of the worst feelings in baseball is losing after you have given everything you've got. All of the Yankees felt this way after losing in seven games to the Pittsburgh Pirates in 1960. The Bronx Bombers had bombed the Bucs for 55 runs and a whopping .338 average, while the world champions had managed just 27 runs and hit at a meager .256 clip. Still, the Pirates hit when they had to, including the ninth-inning homer that delivered the title to the Steel City in the final game. Two Yankees turned in outstanding performances in a losing cause: Bobby Richardson and Mickey Mantle. Although Richardson set a record for RBIs with 12, it was Mantle who truly terrorized the Pirates' pitchers. Time and again he came up in key situations and, despite seeing very few good pitches, hit the ball hard.

In Game Two, Mantle blasted a pair of homers and knocked in five runs in a 16-3 win that evened the series at a game apiece. In Game Three, he went 4 for 5 with another home run to help the Yankees win 10-0. After the Yanks dropped two straight, Mantle came through in Game Six with two runs and two RBIs in a 12-0 blowout.

In Game Seven, Mantle keyed a big sixth inning with a clutch hit off closer Elroy Face, then singled home a huge run in the ninth to help the Yankees tie the score. In the bottom of the inning, he could only watch in despair as Bill Mazeroski's famous homer sailed over the leftfield fence. Mantle's line for the series was spectacular. In 33 plate appearances, he banged out 10 hits and walked 8 times for an on-base average of .545. Mantle scored 8 runs and knocked in 11 with a double and 3 homers. His batting average was .400; his slugging percentage a monstrous .800. Like Ruth in the 1928 World Series, Mantle's performance was all the more remarkable considering that opposing pitchers faced him with one thought in mind: "Don't give him anything good to hit."

the Yankees rallied to tie the game on three singles.

Leading off the bottom of the ninth was Mazeroski, Pittsburgh's eighth-place hitter. No sooner had the Forbes Field crowd caught its breath than Maz turned on Ralph Terry's second pitch and drove it over the leftfield wall to win the World Series. One of the many what-ifs following the series was whether Stengel should have started

Ford in the opening game, which would have enabled Ford to pitch three times. Ford certainly thought so. Yankee management thought so too, and they fired Stengel over the winter.

None of Roger Maris's record-breaking 61 homers was more important than the game-winning shot he hit in Game Three of the 1961 World Series.

> **Pirates 4**
> Best Players: Bill Mazeroski
> (39 errorless chances,
> series-winning HR);
> Roy Face (3 SV)
> **Yankees 3**
> Best Player: Mickey Mantle
> (3 HR, 11 RBIs,
> .485 OBA)

1961
Cincinnati Reds (NL)
vs. New York Yankees (AL)

Once every 25 years or so, a not-so-great team comes together in just the right way and achieves great things. The 1961 Reds were just such a team. Cincy manager Fred Hutchinson built an offense around All-Star outfielders Frank Robinson and Vada Pinson. His pitching staff was anchored by Joey Jay, who finally broke through with 21 wins after making the majors at age 17 in 1953. The rest of the Cincinnati club was made up of role players enjoying excellent seasons at exactly the same time. The Reds won the pennant by four games. The Yankees, meanwhile, had assembled the most awesome power-hitting club in history. Roger Maris broke Babe Ruth's home run record with 61; Mickey Mantle hit 54 before going down with a leg infection in September; and four other Bronx Bombers topped 20 homers. Whitey Ford led the

pitching staff with a 25-4 mark, and Luis Arroyo saved 29 games. A Yankee loss was unthinkable.

The Reds knew they had one chance: to get ahead of the Yankee hitters and make them swing at bad pitches. This strategy worked beautifully in Game One, as Jim O'Toole made just two bad pitches. Unfortunately, Elston Howard and Moose Skowron hit them out of the park, and Ford notched his third straight World Series shutout, 2-0. Jay came in the next afternoon and won 6-2, with key hits from catcher Johnny Edwards and first baseman Gordy Coleman.

Game Three, in Cincinnati, featured a pitching duel between New York's Bill Stafford and veteran Bob Purkey. The Reds were up 2-1 in the eighth, but John Blanchard blasted a pinch-hit homer to tie the game. An inning later, Maris clouted a solo shot to win it. The Yankees very easily could have been in a 3 games to 0 hole, and they knew it. Up 2 games to 1, the New York hitters finally adjusted to Cincinnati's pitching strategy and pounded out 11 hits to win the fourth game 7-0. The barrage continued in Game Five, with the Yanks scoring 11 runs in the first 4 innings to win 13-5.

Yankees 4
  Best Players: Whitey Ford
                 (2-0, 0.00 ERA);
                 Bobby Richardson
                 (.391, 26 errorless
                 chances)
Reds 1
  Best Player: Joey Jay
                (Game 2 victory)

1962
San Francisco Giants (NL) vs. New York Yankees (AL)

Though not as strong as in years past, the Yankees faced no major challenges in 1962 and won the AL pennant by five games. Young Ralph Terry blossomed into a 23-game winner; Whitey Ford had another good year; and Bill Stafford was the "best of the rest" in manager Ralph Houk's patchwork pitching staff. No Yankee batter had a dominant year, although Mickey Mantle—battling a sore knee—slugged .605 and won the MVP award. The Giants, by contrast, looked like they could beat anyone after defeating the Dodgers in a dramatic three-game playoff. Willie Mays, who scored the pennant-winning run, led an offense that featured power hitters Orlando Cepeda, Willie McCovey, and Felipe Alou. San Francisco's pitching staff was deep, with starters Jack Sanford, Billy O'Dell, Billy Pierce, and Juan Marichal combining for 77 wins.

Ford befuddled the Giants in the opener 6-2, but Sanford beat Terry in Game Two with a 2-0 shutout. The series shifted to Yankee Stadium, where Stafford pitched a masterful game and his teammates scratched out three runs against Pierce to win 3-2. The Giants bounced back in Game Four and took a two-run lead behind Marichal, but disaster struck when the 24-year-old Dominican injured his hand while bunting in the fifth inning. The Yankees tied the game against reliever Bobby Bolin, but San Francisco rallied for five runs against Jim Coates and Marshall Bridges to win 7-3 and tie the series. Game Five went to New York, as rookie Tom Tresh crashed a three-run homer in the eighth to give Terry a 5-3 victory.

Three days of rain delayed the conclusion of the series, but this enabled managers Houk and Alvin Dark to send out their best pitchers for the final two games. The Giants beat up on Ford in Game Six, winning 5-2. Game Seven was a classic, with New York scoring a lone run against Sanford on a double play and Terry limiting San Francisco to just two hits heading into the ninth inning. Pinch hitter Matty Alou beat out a bunt, then Terry struck out Felipe Alou and Chuck Hiller. Mays doubled, but rightfielder Roger Maris got to the ball quickly to hold Alou at third. The next batter, McCovey, hit a bullet right at second baseman Bobby Richardson to end the World Series. Had the ball been smashed a few feet either way, two runs would have scored, and the Giants—not the Yankees—would have been world champions.

Willie McCovey's series-ending lineout ranks among the most heart-stopping moments in baseball history.

Yankees 4
Best Players: Ralph Terry
(2 W, Game 7 shutout);
Tom Tresh
(9 H, 1 HR)
Giants 3
Best Player: Jack Sanford (3 quality
starts, 1.93 ERA)

1963
Los Angeles Dodgers (NL) vs. New York Yankees (AL)

The Dodgers had baseball's best pitching and most aggressive offense—as well as a score to settle with the Yankees, who had beaten them six times in seven previous World Series meetings. L.A.'s Sandy Koufax finally fulfilled his immense potential, winning 25 games, striking out 306, and recording more shutouts (11) in one season than anyone in 47 years. Maury Wills,

Junior Gilliam, Willie Davis, Tommy Davis, and big Frank Howard were masters at producing runs, and Koufax, Don Drysdale, and Johnny Podres were among the stingiest starters in baseball. The Yankees had revamped their pitching staff, adding young flame-throwers Al Downing and Jim Bouton to 24-game winner Whitey Ford. The offense was led by Mickey Mantle, Roger Maris, Tom Tresh, rookie Joe Pepitone, and MVP Elston Howard.

Yankee Stadium was packed with 69,000 fans, who watched Koufax retire the first five batters he faced on strikes. Meanwhile, Moose Skowron—traded by the Yanks to the Dodgers before the season—got L.A. on the board with a single against Ford. Two batters later, Johnny Roseboro slammed a three-run homer. Koufax finished with 15 strikeouts to break the old World Series record, beating New York 5-2. The Dodgers got a pair of first-inning runs on a Willie Davis double in Game Two, and Podres made them stand up, tantalizing the Yankees with curves and change-ups in a 4-1 win.

Two days later, the series resumed in Los Angeles. Again, the Dodgers scored early, nicking Bouton for a run in the first. Drysdale gave up just three hits and fanned nine in a 1-0 thriller, and suddenly the mighty Yankees were in an impossible hole. Koufax and Ford hooked up again in Game Four. Ford gave up a solo homer to Frank Howard, but Mantle homered for the Yanks to tie the game in the seventh. Gilliam led off the bottom of the inning with a grounder to third baseman Clete Boyer, who threw the ball low. Pepitone, trying to scoop it out of the dirt, watched helplessly as the ball took a weird bounce, deflected off his wrist, and went up into the stands as Gilliam got to third. Willie Davis drove Gilliam home with a sacrifice fly to center, and the Yanks went down in the ninth for a humiliating sweep.

Dodgers 4
  Best Players: Sandy Koufax (2-0, 23 K)
              Don Drysdale (Game 3 shutout)
Yankees 0
  Best Player: Elston Howard (.333 BA)

1964
St. Louis Cardinals (NL) vs. New York Yankees (AL)

According to the people who ran the Yankees and the Cardinals, neither team had a chance to play in the World Series. St. Louis manager Johnny Keane, his team languishing in fifth place in August, ignored a barrage of criticism from the front office and found a way to mold his team into a surprise contender. Yogi Berra, whose Bronx Bombers had played poorly all summer, lit a fire under his team with an uncharacteristic tirade aimed at a harmonica-playing utility infielder named Phil Linz, and the Yanks suddenly surged past the White Sox and Orioles into first place. New York featured the same familiar faces—Mickey Mantle, Roger Maris, Whitey Ford, Elston Howard, Bobby Richardson, and Tony Kubek—only another year older and another step slower. Three young pitchers hurled them to victory. Mel Stottlemyre, Jim Bouton, and Al Downing won 40 games, and Pedro Ramos saved 8 games down the stretch after being acquired from the Indians in September.

The Cardinals got a boost from Lou Brock, who batted .348 after coming over in a little-noticed deal with the Cubs. Bill White and MVP Ken Boyer provided power from the corners, while catcher Tim McCarver, shortstop Dick Groat, and centerfielder Curt Flood made St. Louis airtight up the middle. The pitching staff was led by Bob Gibson, who came into his own and won 19 games. Ray Sadecki and Curt Simmons rounded out the starting staff, while 37-year-old knuckleballer Barney Schultz gave the bullpen a needed boost. The Cards shot past the Giants and Reds to grab first place after the Phillies collapsed in the final week.

With Mantle limping on a bad knee and Kubek out of action with a sore back, the young Cardinals hoped to ambush the aging Yankees. This they did in the opener, scoring four times in the sixth inning off Ford to give Sadecki and Schultz a lead they would not relinquish, as St. Louis won 9-5. The Yankees took Game Two on run-scoring singles off Gibson by Richardson and Maris, with Stottlemyre claiming the 8-3 victory. Game Three saw Bouton outpitch Simmons for nine innings in a 2-1 game decided by a Mantle homer in the bottom of the ninth. The Cardinals tied the series the next day, when they answered three first-inning New York runs with a grand slam by Boyer to win 4-3.

Gibson returned to the mound for Game Five and fanned 13 batters in 10 innings. He gave up a game-tying homer to Tom Tresh with two out in the ninth, but then shut the Yanks down in the next frame after McCarver belted a three-run blast to make the final score 5-2. The Yankees got to Schultz in Game Six, scoring five times in the eighth inning to blow apart a close game and win 8-3. Game Seven featured a great performance by Gibson, who battled his way through nine tough innings. The Cards

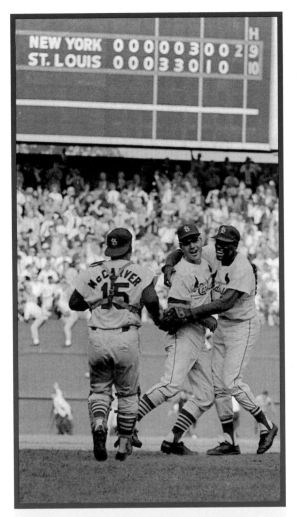

Super-serious Bob Gibson is all smiles after recording the final out of the 1964 World Series. Ken Boyer and Tim McCarver rush to congratulate him.

1965
Los Angeles Dodgers (NL) vs. Minnesota Twins (AL)

For the first time since 1959, the Yankees were a nonfactor in the American League pennant race. This left the door open for the White Sox, the Orioles, and the Twins to battle it out. Solid pitching along with a high-octane attack lifted the Twins to 102 wins and the pennant. Mudcat Grant, Jim Kaat, and Camilo Pascual gave Minnesota an excellent starting staff, while MVP Zoilo Versalles triggered an attack featuring Bob Allison, Harmon Killebrew, and batting champ Tony Oliva.

The Los Angeles lineup was similar to the one that swept the Yankees in 1963. Maury Wills, Junior Gilliam, and Willie Davis got things started, while journeyman Lou Johnson replaced Tommy Davis as the team's power threat after Davis snapped his ankle. The Dodgers' pitching was unbelievable. Sandy Koufax won 26 games and struck out 382 batters; Don Drysdale won 23 times; and Claude Osteen chipped in 15 victories.

The opening game found Koufax out of uniform, in observance of the Jewish holiday Yom Kippur. The Twins got to Drysdale early on a three-run homer by Versalles, and Grant held the Dodgers in check the rest of the way

won 7-5, scoring three times each off Stottlemyre and Downing before adding a final run on Boyer's second home run of the series. No one knew it, but the amazing Yankee dynasty had come to a close. From 1921 to 1964 (a total of 44 Octobers), the team had participated in the World Series 29 times. They would not reach the postseason again for a dozen years.

Sandy Koufax rears back against the Twins in the 1965 World Series. He pitched a shutout on two days' rest in Game Seven.

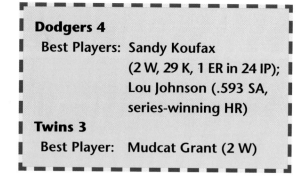

Dodgers 4
Best Players: Sandy Koufax
(2 W, 29 K, 1 ER in 24 IP);
Lou Johnson (.593 SA,
series-winning HR)
Twins 3
Best Player: Mudcat Grant (2 W)

1966
Los Angeles Dodgers (NL) vs. Baltimore Orioles (AL)

The Dodgers employed the same combination of pitching, speed, and defense to win their third pennant in four years. Sandy Koufax was magnificent once again, going 27-9, while the addition of converted starter Phil Regan to the bullpen made L.A. tough to beat in the late innings. The Orioles had pitching, speed, and defense, too. Yet according to the experts, Baltimore lacked the postseason know-how of the Dodgers, and this would be the club's undoing. What the O's did not lack was a menacing force in the middle of the lineup. Rightfielder Frank Robinson, obtained in a trade with the Reds, won the Triple Crown with 49 homers, 122 RBIs, and a .316 average. He was joined by fellow 100-RBI men Brooks Robinson and Boog Powell in a lineup that did not give opposing hurlers much margin for error. The Oriole pitching staff was very young but very talented.

Don Drysdale opened the series for the Dodgers against Dave McNally. Neither lasted past the third inning, and the bullpens took over in a close game. Mop-up man Moe Drabowsky got the Orioles out of a bases-loaded jam and went on to strike out 11 Dodgers in a record-setting relief performance that ended in a surprise 5-2 victory.

for an 8-2 win. Koufax returned for Game Two, but Kaat outpitched him, and the Twins won again, 5-1. The series moved to Los Angeles, where the Dodgers won Game Three 4-0 on a five-hitter by Osteen. L.A. knotted the series the next day, as Drysdale limited the Twins to a pair of bases-empty home runs in a 7-2 romp. The Dodgers took their third straight game 7-0 on a four-hitter by Koufax.

Back in Minneapolis, Grant pitched his second outstanding game of the series despite just two days' rest. He also hit a three-run homer in the 5-1 win to force a seventh game. Game Seven featured Koufax and Kaat, both on two days' rest. The contest was decided by Johnson, who pulled a Kaat pitch down the leftfield line and clanked the ball off the foul pole. The Dodgers scored a second run, and Koufax gave up just two more hits to win 2-0.

The Dodger defense blew Game Two, as centerfielder Willie Davis bungled two fly balls and a weary Koufax could not get past the sixth inning. Jim Palmer, all of 20 years old, spun a four-hit 6-0 shutout for Baltimore.

With the series moving east to Baltimore, it was Wally Bunker's turn to befuddle the Dodgers. The 21-year-old allowed six hits, and Paul Blair blasted a 430-foot (131-m) homer to win 1-0. L.A. manager Walt Alston sent Drysdale back to the hill to restore order in a series that had gotten wildly out of hand for the defending champs. Big Don did just that, allowing just four hits. One of those, however, was a bases-empty home run by Frank Robinson. Incredibly, McNally protected this slim lead, allowing a mere four hits to record Baltimore's third consecutive shutout—and to complete one of the most improbable sweeps in sports history.

> **Orioles 4**
> **Best Players:** Jim Palmer
> (Game 2 shutout);
> Moe Drabowsky
> (6 straight K in Game 1)
> **Dodgers 0**
> **Best Player:** Claude Osteen
> (1 ER in Game 3)

1967
St. Louis Cardinals (NL) vs. Boston Red Sox (AL)

After rising from ninth place to first and winning the AL pennant in a wild final week, the red-hot Red Sox made the outcome of the 1967 World Series difficult to predict. In his first year as a major-league manager, Dick Williams had built a team around Triple Crown winner Carl Yastrzemski and 22-game winner Jim Lonborg with a combination of young players and undistinguished journeyman. The Cardinals, on the other hand, had a star-studded lineup featuring All-Stars Orlando Cepeda, Lou Brock, Tim McCarver, and Bob Gibson. It was a clash of mature, proven stars and adrenaline-pumped kids.

Because Lonborg had pitched on the season's final day, Gibson faced Boston's number-four starter, Jose Santiago. The Puerto Rican native did well, but he lost 2-1 when Brock singled, stole second, and scored on a pair of groundouts. Lonborg knotted the series in Game Two with one of history's finest pitching performances. The lanky right-hander came within four outs of a no-hitter, allowing only an eighth-inning double to Julian Javier in a 5-0 Boston win. Nelson Briles took the mound for St. Louis in Game Three and treated the hometown fans to a 5-2 complete-game victory. The Cardinals took a commanding lead when Gibson hurled a shutout in Game Four.

With their backs against the wall, the young Red Sox surprised the experts by winning Game Five 3-1. Again it was Lonborg to the rescue with another terrific game. With their Fenway Park fans cheering wildly, the Red Sox exploded for six hits and four runs in the seventh inning of Game Six to win 8-4 and force a seventh game. Lonborg returned on three days' rest to face a well-rested Gibson, and it showed. The Cardinals broke through for seven runs in the first six innings, with Javier sending a three-run blast over the Green Monster to put the game out of reach. Gibson struck out ten and homered for the deciding run in a 7-2 win that ended Boston's "Impossible Dream."

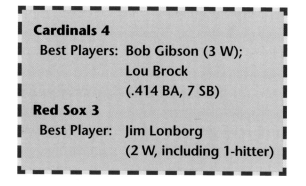

Cardinals 4
  Best Players: Bob Gibson (3 W);
              Lou Brock
              (.414 BA, 7 SB)
Red Sox 3
  Best Player: Jim Lonborg
             (2 W, including 1-hitter)

1968
St. Louis Cardinals (NL) vs. Detroit Tigers (AL)

In a series featuring teams that dominated their respective pennant races, the experts were predicting that hitting, not pitching, would be the deciding factor. The Cardinals and Tigers both had astonishing pitching, but their offenses scored runs in dramatically different ways. St. Louis depended on the speed of Lou Brock and Curt Flood and the clutch hitting of Orlando Cepeda and Mike Shannon. The Tigers, who hit 112 more homers than St. Louis, preferred to sit and wait for the long ball. Their lineup included power hitters Norm Cash, Willie Horton, Al Kaline, Bill Freehan, and Jim Northrup.

Game One matched 31-game winner Denny McLain against Bob Gibson, whose ERA for the Cardinals in 1968 was a microscopic 1.12. Gibson was fantastic, striking out a record 17 Tigers while his teammates scratched out three runs against McLain in a 4-0 victory. Detroit bounced back the next day as Mickey Lolich hit a homer and pitched an 8-1 complete-game win. The Cardinal bats came alive in Detroit, where Cepeda and Tim McCarver blasted three-run homers in a 7-3 Game Three win. St. Louis took Game Four as well, scoring 10 runs for Gibson, who allowed just one. The

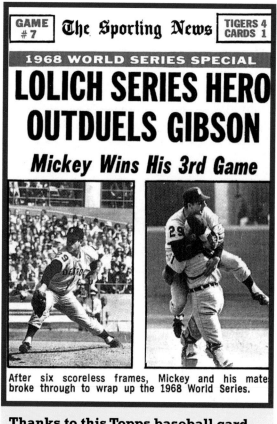

After six scoreless frames, Mickey and his mate broke through to wrap up the 1968 World Series.

Thanks to this Topps baseball card, collectors have been reliving Mickey Lolich's Game Seven heroics for more than 30 years.

Cardinals looked like they would close out the series in five games when Cepeda homered in the first inning of the next contest, but Lolich stopped the scoring there, and the Tigers came back to win 5-3.

Returning to Busch Stadium, the Cardinals were unable to hit McLain in Game Six. The Tigers had no trouble with the St. Louis hurlers, bombing them for ten runs in the third inning to even the series with a 13-1 blowout. Game Seven pitted Lolich against Gibson. Neither team got a man to second through six frames, but the momentum shifted Detroit's way after Lolich picked Brock and Flood off first in the same inning.

In the seventh, Gibson retired the first two batters but gave up two singles. Northrup hit a line drive to Flood, who misplayed the third out into a two-run triple that broke the game open. The Tigers won 4-1 and accomplished that rarest of baseball comebacks, winning a World Series after losing three of the first four games.

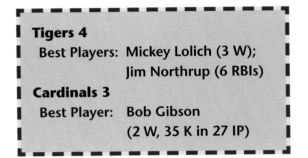

Tigers 4
Best Players: Mickey Lolich (3 W);
Jim Northrup (6 RBIs)
Cardinals 3
Best Player: Bob Gibson
(2 W, 35 K in 27 IP)

1969
New York Mets (NL) vs. Baltimore Orioles (AL)

The 1969 National League pennant winners may have been called the "Miracle Mets," but there was nothing miraculous about how they got to the World Series—pitching, defense, clutch hitting, and cool, intelligent managing. Gil Hodges molded a group of talented youngsters into a strong and confident club that featured the one-two pitching punch of Tom Seaver and Jerry Koosman, as well as highly effective platoons at four of the eight field positions. The Orioles were almost identical to the 1966 championship club, but they had added 23-game winner Mike Cuellar and improved their defense in a couple of spots. The Orioles did not have a visible weakness and thus were expected to crush the young Mets.

Game One offered no reason to argue with this expectation. The Orioles jumped on Seaver early, with Don Buford homering in the first and three more runs scoring in the fourth. Cuellar cruised to a 4-1 win. In Game Two, the Mets found the key to beating Baltimore: lights-out pitching by Koosman, who gave up just two singles in just under nine innings. Game Three, in New York, changed the entire tone of the series. The Orioles were helpless against a pair of 22-year-olds named Gary Gentry and Nolan Ryan. Their fastballs exploded over the plate and completely overpowered the powerful Orioles. Two eye-popping catches by centerfielder Tommie Agee preserved a 4-0 victory.

Seaver returned to the mound for Game Four and held the Orioles scoreless until the ninth. With one out and two men on, Brooks Robinson lined a ball to rightfield. Ron Swoboda, one of the Mets' poorest defenders, made an incredible diving catch that sent the game into extra innings. In the bottom of the tenth, J.C. Martin bunted and was hit in the back by the throw, allowing pinch runner Rod Gaspar to score the winning run for New York. In Game Five, Baltimore took a 3-0 lead on homers by Frank Robinson and Dave McNally but got just one more hit the rest of the way. The Mets pulled ahead on a Swoboda double in the eighth, and Koosman went the distance to give the Mets an unforgettable world title.

Mets 4
Best Players: Donn Clendenon
(3 HR, 1.071 SA);
Jerry Koosman
(2-0, 2.04 ERA)
Orioles 1
Best Player: Mike Cuellar
(1-0, 1.13 ERA)

CHAPTER 9

THE 1970s

1970
Cincinnati Reds (NL) vs. Baltimore Orioles (AL)

The Orioles rolled through the regular season and playoffs the same way they had in 1969—with good hitting, great pitching, and extraordinary defense. This time they faced a National League opponent that counted less on miracles and more on pounding their opponents into submission. Cincinnati's "Big Red Machine" featured clutch-hitting Tony Perez, MVP Johnny Bench, and slugger Lee May batting behind two exceptional table-setters, Pete Rose and Bobby Tolan. To stop them, the Orioles would count on 20-game winners Dave McNally, Mike Cuellar, and Jim Palmer. Pitching was not the Reds' strong point. Injuries to Jim Maloney and Jim Merritt left first-year manager Sparky Anderson scrambling to field a respectable starting staff.

Game One, at Riverfront Stadium in Cincinnati, was the first World Series contest ever played on artificial turf. The Reds looked right at home, scoring a first-inning run and then adding two more on a laser over the leftfield fence by May. The Orioles tied the game on a pair of homers, and then Brooks Robinson robbed May of a double

with a miraculous diving stop and throw from third base. Robinson put the Orioles in front with a solo homer in the seventh, and that is where they stayed for a 4-3 win. Game Two went to the Orioles, too, as they erased a 4-0 Cincinnati lead and prevailed 6-5.

The series moved to Baltimore, where the Orioles bombed Cincy pitchers for ten runs. Brooks Robinson crushed the Reds'

Brooks Robinson robs Johnny Bench in Game Three of the 1970 World Series. His remarkable glovework earned Robinson the series MVP award.

spirit with a trio of unbelievable fielding plays, and McNally personally outscored the entire Cincinnati team, hitting a grand slam in a 9-3 victory. With all hope seemingly lost, the Reds rebounded from a 5-3 deficit in Game Four when May launched a three-run homer to give his team its first win, 6-5. Reds fans got their hopes up briefly in Game Five when Rose, Bench, and May came around to score in the opening inning. But Cuellar held the Reds to two hits the rest of the way, and the Orioles answered with nine runs to cruise to the world championship that had slipped through their fingers in 1969.

> **Orioles 4**
> Best Players: Brooks Robinson
>   (.429 BA, great defense)
>   Paul Blair
>   (.474 BA, 9 R)
> **Reds 1**
> Best Player: Lee May
>   (.389 BA, 8 RBIs)

1971
Pittsburgh Pirates (NL) vs. Baltimore Orioles (AL)

Pitching wins pennants. The Orioles proved this in 1971 by taking their division by 12 games and then easily disposing of the A's in the American League Championship Series (ALCS). Baltimore had four 20-game winners in Dave McNally, Mike Cuellar, Jim Palmer, and Pat Dobson, and a good reliever in Eddie Watt. The Orioles' offense still revolved around Boog Powell, Frank Robinson, Brooks Robinson, and leadoff man Don Buford. The Pirates reached the

World Series using a similar formula, with a staff led by Dock Ellis, Steve Blass, Nelson Briles, young Bruce Kison—who was called up on July 4 and won 9 of 12 decisions—and Dave Giusti, whose 30 saves led the league. The Pittsburgh hitters were a free-swinging bunch led by NL home-run champion Willie Stargell and Roberto Clemente, who hit .341 in the 17th year of his glorious career. The Pirates were underdogs, but after beating the powerful Reds in the National League Championship Series (NLCS), they were swelling with confidence.

The Orioles recovered from a shaky start in Game One to win 5-3 behind McNally's three-hitter and homers by outfielders Buford, Frank Robinson, and Merv Rettenmund. The Orioles won with ease in the second game of the series by pounding out 14 hits in an 11-3 win for Palmer. When the teams met again in Pittsburgh the next day, Blass stifled the Orioles and got Pittsburgh back on the winning track, 5-1. The following evening marked the first night game in World Series history, and the Pirates battled furiously to overcome three early Baltimore runs. Kison pitched well in relief, and pinch hitter Milt May singled home the winning run in the seventh inning to even the series for Pittsburgh. Briles hurled a 4-0 shutout in Game Five to send the Orioles back to Baltimore down a game and facing elimination.

In Game Six, the Orioles scrapped their way into extra innings with runs in the sixth and seventh. Frank Robinson hustled home in the tenth on a short fly by Brooks Robinson to win it for Baltimore 3-2 and force a seventh game. Blass and Cuellar faced off in one of the most exciting games of the era. With both pitchers throwing well, it was the old-timer Clemente who made the difference. His two-out solo home run in the fourth gave the Pirates a 1-0 lead, and they won 2-1 on Blass's four-hitter.

Pirates 4
Best Players: Steve Blass
(2-0, 1.00 ERA);
Roberto Clemente
(.414 BA, 5 XBH)
Orioles 3
Best Player: Brooks Robinson
(.318 BA, 5 RBIs)

1972
Cincinnati Reds (NL)
vs. Oakland A's (AL)

The Oakland A's, winners of 101 games in 1971, seemed ready to assume their place at the top of the AL. The only thing that stood in the team's way was the team itself. Thanks to erratic owner Charles Finley, no-nonsense manager Dick Williams, and ego-tistical superstar Reggie Jackson, the A's clubhouse was rarely a calm or quiet place. Still, they won enough games to stay ahead of the White Sox and had good enough pitching to get past the Tigers in the ALCS. Oakland's rotation of Catfish Hunter, Ken Holtzman, Blue Moon Odom, and Vida Blue was the finest in baseball. The bullpen, anchored by Rollie Fingers, was unhittable. Oakland also had speed in shortstop Bert Campaneris and enough clutch hitting in Jackson, Joe Rudi, and Sal Bando to win the close ones.

Oakland's opponents, the Cincinnati Reds, had improved themselves immensely by trading Lee May for second baseman Joe Morgan. He joined with Pete Rose and Bobby Tolan to give the Reds three terrific table-setters for sluggers Johnny Bench and Tony Perez. Gary Nolan led a patchwork pitching staff designed to deliver leads to relief stars Pedro Borbon and Clay Carroll, who combined for 48 saves. With Jackson unavailable to the A's because of a leg injury, the Reds were given a slight edge in this series.

That edge disappeared in the fifth inning of Game One, when Gene Tenace, a backup catcher with a .225 average, crushed his second home run of the day off Nolan to give Oakland a 3-2 win. Game Two was a one-man show by Hunter, who stymied the Reds and singled in the deciding run in a 2-1

Catfish Hunter did it all in his Game Two victory over the Reds, including driving home the winning run.

victory. The A's, heading to Oakland with a two-game bulge, now had a huge advantage. Cincinnati starter Jack Billingham got the Reds halfway back with a 1-0 shutout in Game Three. The Reds appeared to have evened up the series in Game Four as they reached the ninth inning with a 2-1 lead, but the A's stunned them with a pair of runs to win 3-2. Once again, Tenace was a key player, hitting a fifth-inning home run and scoring the game winner after singling against Carroll.

With their backs against the wall, the Reds pulled out a 5-4 win in the ninth inning of Game Five, then trounced the A's 8-1 back in Cincinnati. It was the only game of the series not decided by one run. Game Seven went to the A's, 3-2, with Tenace doubling home the go-ahead run in the sixth inning and Fingers finishing off the Reds in the ninth.

> **A's 4**
> Best Players: Gene Tenace
> (4 HR, 9 RBIs);
> Catfish Hunter
> (2-0, 2.81 ERA)
> **Reds 3**
> Best Player: Jack Billingham
> (2 starts, 0.00 ERA)

1973
New York Mets (NL) vs. Oakland A's (AL)

The A's came into the World Series hoping to be the first back-to-back winners since the 1962 Yankees. Their pitching was even better than in 1972, with Catfish Hunter, Ken Holtzman, and Vida Blue winning 20 or more games each. Reggie Jackson had an MVP year with a league-high 32 homers and 117 RBIs, while Sal Bando and 1972 World Series hero Gene Tenace both topped 20 home runs. In addition to Bert Campaneris, the A's had another stolen base threat in centerfielder Billy North, who swiped 53 bases. On paper, this series looked like a wipeout. The Mets had won their division with a meager 82-79 record, and they did not have one healthy, high-quality hitter in the lineup. Their only real hope was pitching, which had saved them against the Reds in the NLCS. Tom Seaver, Jerry Koosman, and Jon Matlack had shut down the Big Red Machine, allowing less than two earned runs a game. How this trio did against the A's would likely decide the series.

Matlack did better against the A's in the opener than Koosman did in Game Two. Surprisingly, though, the A's won Game One 2-1 behind Holtzman and lost a day later 10-7 when the Mets scored four times in a tumultuous 12th inning. Three of those runs scored on a pair of errors by backup infielder Mike Andrews. A's owner Charles Finley was so infuriated that he tried to fire Andrews after the game, but he was stopped by commissioner Bowie Kuhn. The series moved to Oakland, where the A's prevailed in another extra-inning game, 3-2. The Mets made it 2-all by winning Game Four 6-1 on a three-run homer by Rusty Staub, who was playing through the pain of a partially dislocated shoulder. New York won again on a 2-0 shutout by Koosman and Tug McGraw to take a one-game lead in the series.

The two games in Oakland showed why the A's were champions. Twice in the first three innings of Game Six, Jackson faced

Seaver with men on base, and twice he doubled home runs. With Hunter shutting down the Mets, that was all Oakland needed. The A's won 3-1. In Game Seven, Jackson and Campaneris homered to give Holtzman a 4-0 lead. He made it stand up with help from Darold Knowles, who got a save in his seventh series appearance. Oakland won 5-2. The mark of a great team is how they play when they are not playing their best. For the second straight October, Oakland was outpitched and outscored, yet they won again.

> **A's 4**
> **Best Players:** Reggie Jackson
> (winning H in
> Games 6 and 7);
> Ken Holtzman
> (2 W)
> **Mets 3**
> **Best Player:** Rusty Staub
> (.423 BA, 6 RBIs)

1974
Los Angeles Dodgers (NL) vs. Oakland A's (AL)

Ever since the American League expanded into California in the 1960s, West Coast fans knew that it was only a matter of time before they would be treated to an all-California World Series. This came to pass in 1974, when the A's won their third straight pennant despite off years from a few key players and a new manager, Alvin Dark. Catfish Hunter had a great season, with 25 wins and a 2.49 ERA, and the bullpen was excellent as usual. The Dodgers took the pennant on the strength of their great young infield of Ron Cey, Bill Russell,

Davey Lopes, and Steve Garvey, who won the MVP. Additional firepower came from outfielder Jim Wynn and the catching platoon of Steve Yeager and Joe Ferguson. What put L.A. over the top, however, was its trade for reliever Mike Marshall. Marshall pitched in a record 106 games, winning 15 and saving 21. Don Sutton and Andy Messersmith led a rotation that had lost Tommy John to a devastating midseason elbow injury but was still very capable.

Sloppy defense and pitching by the Dodgers gave the A's an opening in Game One, and they took it, winning 3-2 despite being out-hit 11-6. L.A. won by the same score in Game Two. The key blow was a two-run homer by Ferguson off starter Vida Blue. The series moved north to Oakland, where yet another 3-2 game was won by the A's, who survived late homers by Bill Buckner and Willie Crawford.

Oakland starter Ken Holtzman helped himself with a solo homer to open the scoring in Game Four, but Russell answered that blow with a two-run triple to give the Dodgers a lead in the fourth inning. In the turning point of the series, L.A. wasted a chance to widen its advantage in the sixth inning when Garvey, Ferguson, and Cey failed to hit after Wynn pumped out a lead-off double. Sensing the kill, the A's tallied four runs in the bottom of the inning and went on to win 5-2. Incredibly, the teams played a fourth 3-2 game the next day, with Oakland coming out on top and winning the series. With the score tied 2-2 in the seventh, Joe Rudi drilled Mike Marshall's first delivery into the leftfield stands, and that was that. In a very close "one-sided" series, the A's became the first team since the Yankees of the early 1950s to win three world championships in a row.

A's 4
Best Players: Rollie Fingers (1 W, 2 SV);
Joe Rudi (.333 BA,
series-winning HR)
Dodgers 1
Best Player: Don Sutton
(1-0, 2.77 ERA)

1975
Cincinnati Reds (NL)
vs. Boston Red Sox (AL)

After eight years of trades, injuries, and retirements, all that was left of the 1967 Red Sox were Carl Yastrzemski and Rico Petrocelli. The two former stars were now secondary contributors to the Boston offense, which was powered by two phenomenal rookies, Fred Lynn and Jim Rice. They were joined by young veterans Carlton Fisk, Denny Doyle, Bernie Carbo, Cecil Cooper, Rick Burleson, and Dwight Evans. The Red Sox pitching staff featured rock-solid Rick Wise and noted eccentrics Luis Tiant and Bill Lee.

Cincinnati had a monster offense built, as always, around Pete Rose, Joe Morgan, Tony Perez, and Johnny Bench. Now they were joined by two more accomplished hitters, George Foster and Ken Griffey. Sparky Anderson's pitching formula still focused on relief pitching—in this case, Pedro Borbon, Clay Carroll, Rawley Eastwick, and Will McEnaney. The starting staff was not bad, however, with veterans Don Gullett, Gary Nolan, Jack Billingham, and Fred Norman. If there was an obvious advantage in this series, it belonged to the Reds because they would not have to deal with Rice, who was out with a bad wrist.

The Big Red Machine came to a grinding halt when it encountered Tiant in Game One. He completely befuddled the Cincinnati hitters with his weird assortment of pitches, speeds, and deliveries—sometimes spinning all the way around to face centerfield before flinging the ball toward the plate. The Reds recovered from their 6-0 Game One defeat the next day, when they scored a 3-2 comeback with hits off reliever Dick Drago in the ninth. Game Three, in Cincinnati, was another close one, with the Reds prevailing in the bottom of the tenth on a bases-loaded hit by Morgan. The contest featured six home runs, including a dramatic game-tying shot by Evans in the ninth. Boston knotted the series in Game Four with a five-run outburst in the fourth inning. Tiant, who scored the fifth run, held on for a 5-4 win. Game Five went to the Reds, who got a pair of homers from Perez in an easy 6-2 victory.

Reds 4
Best Players: Pete Rose (.370 BA);
Tony Perez (3 HR in
Games 5 and 7)
Red Sox 3
Best Player: Luis Tiant (2-0)

Three days of rain delayed the start of Game Six in Fenway Park. This heightened the tension and enabled the managers to rest their best pitchers. Tiant and Nolan took the mound when the rain stopped, but they were long gone when Carbo saved the Red Sox with a three-run pinch-hit homer to tie the game in the eighth. In the bottom of the 12th, Fisk came to the plate against Pat Darcy and homered just inside the leftfield

BEST GAME:
GAME SIX, 1975 WORLD SERIES

America waited and waited and waited for Game Six of the 1975 World Series. A day of travel plus three rainouts turned what should have been an easy win for the Reds into a Cincinnati nightmare. Only one Boston pitcher, Luis Tiant, proved capable of shutting down the Big Red Machine, and he had thrown his heart out in Game Four. But with every rainy day, Tiant grew stronger—and so did the hopes of fans throughout New England.

When Game Six finally began, Tiant took the mound against Gary Nolan. The Red Sox staked their ace to a 3-0 lead in the first inning when Fred Lynn hit a three-run bomb to right. Four innings later, a hushed Fenway Park crowd watched as Lynn lay motionless on the turf. He had just slammed into the wall chasing Ken Griffey's two-run triple, and he looked like he was through. After several minutes with the team trainer, Lynn convinced him that he was okay to stay in the game. The happiness of Boston fans turned quickly though, when Johnny Bench rifled a ball off the Green Monster to score Griffey and tie the game 3-3.

The Reds continued to hit Tiant. George Foster doubled home a pair of runs in the seventh, and Cesar Geronimo homered to lead off the eighth and give Cincinnati a 6-3 lead. Sparky Anderson called in his bullpen to finish off the game, but Boston put two runners on in the bottom of the eighth. Closer Rawley Eastwick came in and quickly retired Dwight Evans and Rick Burleson to bring up the pitcher's spot. Bernie Carbo, a former Red, pinch-hit and worked Eastwick to a 3-2 count. After fouling off a good pitch, Carbo drilled a fantastic homer to dead centerfield to make the score 6-6.

For the next four innings, the pressure was excruciating. The Red Sox loaded the bases in the ninth with no one out but could not score, as Lynn flied out to left-fielder George Foster, who nailed Denny Doyle at the plate. In the top of the 11th, Joe Morgan was robbed of a two-run homer in the rightfield corner by Dwight Evans, who then doubled up Griffey, who was running from first on the play. Two

foul pole to win one of the most dramatic games in World Series history. With an enormous television audience tuning in the next evening, the Reds erased a 3-0 deficit with the help of another Perez home run, then won the game 4-3 on Morgan's ninth-inning bloop single.

1976
Cincinnati Reds (NL) vs. New York Yankees (AL)

As good as the Reds were in 1975, they were even better in 1976. They had more hits, runs, extra-base hits, and stolen bases, singles went to waste for the Reds in the 12th inning, and this gave Boston the chance it needed. With Pat Darcy on the mound, leadoff hitter Carlton Fisk crushed the first pitch he saw high and deep down the leftfield line. Fisk watched as his hit began to curve foul and tried to "wave" it fair. The ball landed just to the right of the foul pole for a game-winning home run.

Obviously, Game Six was huge for the Red Sox. But it was just as big for baseball. Pro football had been gaining in popularity and, some maintained, had surpassed baseball as America's national pastime. The previous evening, when the game was pushed back for a third straight day because of rain, a lot of reporters felt that the league made the decision to cancel for reasons other than poor playing conditions. It was a Monday evening, and ABC's *Monday Night Football* was on. To this day there are those who believe the game was called because commissioner Bowie Kuhn was afraid that, head-to-head, a regular-season football game would have outdrawn a World Series baseball game. Everything worked out for the best, however, when some 70 million people tuned in to watch Game Six on Tuesday night. Never before had so many sports fans witnessed such a good game. As a result, enthusiasm for baseball remained high throughout the 1970s.

Carlton Fisk celebrates his 12th-inning home run against the Reds. Game Six of the 1975 World Series remains unmatched for drama and intensity.

while hitting for a much higher average. George Foster emerged as a big star, with 29 homers and a league-best 121 RBIs, while Joe Morgan won his second straight MVP award. At 35, Pete Rose had one of his best seasons ever, leading the NL with 130 runs, 215 hits, and 42 doubles. The Reds' pitching was deep for a change, with six capable starters and the usual lights-out bullpen.

The Yankees, back in the Fall Classic for the first time since the days of Maris and Mantle, combined the pitching of celebrated free agent Catfish Hunter, Ed Figueroa,

Dock Ellis, and Sparky Lyle with the clutch hitting of MVP Thurman Munson, home-run leader Graig Nettles, and Chris Chambliss, whose dramatic homer had won the ALCS a couple of days earlier.

Cincinnati's Don Gullett gave up a first-inning run and then pitched well the rest of the way in Game One, combining with Pedro Borbon for a 5-1 win. Game Two appeared to be headed for extra innings until New York's Fred Stanley threw Ken Griffey's grounder away with two outs in the ninth inning, and the score was tied 2-2. Griffey came around to score the game winner on Tony Perez's single.

The Yankees' luck did not change on their home field, where the Reds hammered out four hits and stole two bases in a three-run second inning against Dock Ellis. Young Pat Zachry and Will McEnaney finished off the Yanks 6-2. Game Four was no better for New York, as Johnny Bench clubbed a two-run homer to give the Reds a 3-1 lead. Cincinnati put the game away in the ninth, when Bench homered again. The Reds won 7-2 to complete an impressive sweep.

Reds 4
Best Players: Johnny Bench
(.533 BA, 4 XBH);
Joe Morgan (.333 BA,
2 SB, 3 XBH)
Yankees 0
Best Player: Thurman Munson
(.529 BA, 6 straight H
in Games 3 and 4)

Johnny Bench destroyed Yankee pitching in the 1976 World Series, batting .533 and smashing a pair of homers in the final game.

1977
Los Angeles Dodgers (NL) vs. New York Yankees (AL)

After watching his team getting swept in 1976, New York owner George Steinbrenner opened his wallet over the winter and signed free agents Reggie Jackson and Don Gullett. Despite adding these two stars, the Yankees barely outpaced the Orioles and Red Sox in the Eastern Division. In the ALCS, New York needed a gritty comeback to beat the Royals. Thus, by the time they met the Dodgers, they were a hardened bunch. The Los Angeles team that took the field was similar to the 1974 pennant winner. The same great infield was intact; Steve Yeager was still behind the plate; and pitchers Don Sutton, Doug Rau, and Tommy John were big winners. But the Dodgers had a much-improved outfield of Dusty Baker, Bill Buckner, and Reggie Smith, and had added Rick Rhoden and Burt Hooton to the starting staff. Gone, however, was Mike

BEST GAME BY A HITTER: REGGIE JACKSON, 1977

When Reggie Jackson starred for the Oakland A's in the early 1970s, he used to joke that if he played in New York, they would name a candy bar after him. Well, they did. The Reggie Bar made its Yankee Stadium debut the same day Jackson did, in April 1977. When he homered in that game, Reggie Bars rained down from the stands in tribute to the Yankees' newly signed slugger. Owner George Steinbrenner hired Jackson to do one thing: win the World Series. It is unwise to put that kind of pressure on a single player. But if there was one player who was willing to shoulder that responsibility, it was the man they called "Mr. October." When October rolled around, Mr. October was ready to roll.

Reggie Jackson launches his third home run against the Dodgers in Game Six of the 1977 World Series.

The Yankees and Dodgers were very evenly matched. After a split of the first two games in New York, the series moved to Los Angeles, where the Yankees beat the Dodgers in Games Three and Four. Down 3 games to 1, the Dodgers clobbered the Yankees 10-4 and regained some momentum.

Game Six, back in New York, started badly for the Yankees. After Mike Torrez retired the first two Dodgers, he allowed two base runners on an error and a walk. Steve Garvey, L.A.'s top hitter, belted a line drive into the rightfield corner, and both runners scored. New York tied the score in the second inning, but the Dodgers hung tough, scoring again in the third to retake the lead.

Thurman Munson led off the fourth inning with a single. Then Jackson hammered Hooton's first delivery into the rightfield stands. The Yanks scored another run to make the score 5-3. With two out in the fifth, Jackson came to the plate against reliever Elias Sosa. Once again, Jackson blasted the first pitch into the rightfield stands for a two-run homer. The shell-shocked Dodgers were now down 7-3.

L.A. regrouped in the next two innings and kept the Yankees from scoring. In the eighth, however, knuckle-baller Charlie Hough had to deal with Jackson. For the third time in a row, Reggie swung at the first pitch he saw and hit it out of the park. This eye-popping blast landed in the seats in the farthest reaches of centerfield.

Many other players have had great World Series games, but no one ever did so much under so much pressure. Jackson's three home runs not only tied the record set by Babe Ruth during the 1920s, but also established a new mark of five home runs during the course of a World Series.

Marshall, who had been dealt to the Braves in 1975. Though knuckle-baller Charlie Hough and Mike Garman did a decent job closing games, the Dodger bullpen was definitely its weakness.

Willie Randolph, New York's 23-year-old All-Star second baseman, was the difference in the opener. His sixth-inning homer tied the score at 2-2, and he doubled and scored to win the game in the bottom of the 12th. The Dodgers shook off this disappointment and trounced the Yankees 6-1 in Game Two, as Hooton fired a five-hitter at the New Yorkers and L.A. got homers from Yeager, Smith, Ron Cey, and Steve Garvey. Pitching a complete game for the Yankees when the series shifted to Los Angeles, Mike Torrez allowed only a three-run homer to Baker in a 5-3 win. The Yankees took a commanding lead in the series by winning Game Four 4-2 behind Ron Guidry, who also went the distance.

Down 3 games to 1, the Dodgers survived back-to-back home runs by Thurman Munson and Jackson to win 10-4 in Game Five. Game Six, back in New York, started well for Los Angeles but ended badly. After scoring twice in the first inning and once more in the third, they lost the lead when Jackson lofted a homer into the rightfield seats for his third round-tripper in three games. But "Mr. October" was just getting started. In the next inning, Jackson pulled an Elias Sosa pitch into the stands for his second home run of the night. Up 7-3, the Yankees added a final run on Jackson's third home run of the game, which had been a mammoth blast off Hough to centerfield. The Yanks won 8-4 to claim their first world championship since 1962.

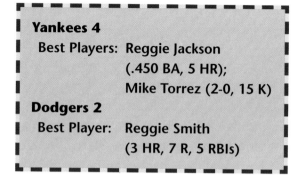

Yankees 4
 Best Players: Reggie Jackson
                (.450 BA, 5 HR);
                Mike Torrez (2-0, 15 K)
Dodgers 2
 Best Player: Reggie Smith
               (3 HR, 7 R, 5 RBIs)

1978
Los Angeles Dodgers (NL) vs. New York Yankees (AL)

In any other year, baseball fans would have been buzzing about L.A.'s great comeback from 6.5 games down to win their division. But the Yankees had outdone them. The Bronx Bombers had been as far as 14 games back, beaten the Red Sox in a one-game divisional playoff, and then erased leads in the final two games of the ALCS to defeat the Royals for the third year in a row. The Dodgers were looking for revenge after being humiliated in the final game of the 1977 World Series. The Yankees were just looking for a chance to catch their breath.

Game One saw the Dodgers batter four Yankee pitchers to win 11-5. Then Burt Hooton beat Catfish Hunter in Game Two, which ended with two Yankees on base. With one down in the ninth and L.A. up 4-3, rookie Bob Welch had to retire Thurman Munson and Reggie Jackson to close out the game. Munson flied out, but Jackson worked Welch to a full count. Swinging from the heels, the slugger fouled off four fastballs before striking out, and the Yankees returned to the Bronx down 2 games to 0.

Ron Guidry, 25-3 during the season, took the mound for New York and was hit hard by the Dodger righties. He was saved by third baseman Graig Nettles, who made four eye-popping plays to snuff out L.A. rallies. Guidry triumphed 5-1 despite allowing 16 hitters to reach base. With the momentum suddenly turned, the Yankees won 4-3 in ten innings on a Lou Piniella single off Welch. Game Five began well for the Dodgers, who took a 2-0 lead. But the Yankee bats awoke for 18 hits, and the Bronx Bombers won 12-2 to take a 3-2 series lead. Back in L. A., the discombobulated Dodgers allowed Dent and substitute second baseman Brian Doyle to get six hits and five RBIs, and Jackson slugged a long opposite-field homer against Welch to leave his mark on the World Series for the second straight year. The Yankees' 7-2 win marked the first time a team had ever lost the first two games and then come back to win four in a row.

> **Yankees 4**
> **Best Players: Bucky Dent**
> **(10 H, 7 RBIs);**
> **Thurman Munson**
> **(7 RBIs in 4 New**
> **York W)**
> **Dodgers 2**
> **Best Player: Tommy John**
> **(5 ER in 2 starts)**

1979
Pittsburgh Pirates (NL) vs. Baltimore Orioles (AL)

Who said you can't remake your infield in the middle of the year? Certainly Pittsburgh manager Chuck Tanner never believed this. In 1979, he acquired veterans Tim Foli and Bill Madlock in trades and made Phil Garner his everyday second baseman. They combined with 38-year-old Willie Stargell to give the Pirates a brand-new look. This adjustment was just enough to get Pittsburgh past the Montreal Expos, who finished two games back in the Eastern Division. The Pirates then swept the Reds in the NLCS on the strength of their pitching, which included veterans Bert Blyleven, Jim Bibby, John Candelaria, and Kent Tekulve. A close-knit team that looked up to Stargell as a father figure, the Pirates were far greater than the sum of their parts. The Orioles returned to the top of the AL East on the arm of 23-game winner Mike Flanagan, the bats of MVP runner-up Ken Singleton and young slugger Eddie Murray, and the leadoff skills of Al Bumbry. Baltimore manager Earl Weaver liked to play for the "big inning" and wait for two- and three-run homers. He had a good team with which to pursue this strategy. The O's had plenty of punch and enough of everything else to get by.

Game One began with a Baltimore bang, as the Orioles chased Bruce Kison from the game with five first-inning runs. Flanagan went all the way for the 5-4 win. The Pirates bounced back to win Game Two 3-2 with a tie-breaking run in the ninth. The series moved to Pittsburgh, where the Orioles started hitting again and Scott McGregor pitched a complete game 8-4 victory. Game Four saw the Orioles dig themselves out of a 6-3 hole with six runs in the eighth inning off closer Tekulve.

Down 3 games to 1 with two of the final three games scheduled for Baltimore, the Pirates were in quite a hole themselves. They had hit and pitched as well as they could, and yet had just a single win to show for it. Their talent and team spirit finally came out in Game Five, when Jim Rooker and Blyleven combined on a six-hitter to

Willie Stargell jumps for joy after recording the final out of the 1979 World Series. He led the Pirates to victory with a two-run homer in Game Seven.

beat the Orioles 7-1. Game Six featured a gem by Candelaria and Tekulve, who shut out Baltimore 4-0 to force a seventh game. Team leader Stargell took charge in the dramatic finale, erasing a 1-0 Orioles lead with a two-run homer. The Pirates added two more runs in the ninth, and Tekulve slammed the door on Baltimore to cap an inspiring comeback. For just the fourth time, a team survived a 1-3 start to win it all.

Pirates 4
  Best Players: Willie Stargell
                (12 H, 3 HR);
                Kent Tekulve (3 SV)
Orioles 3
  Best Player: Kiko Garcia
                (.400 BA, 6 RBIs)

CHAPTER 10

THE 1980s

1980
Philadelphia Phillies (NL)
vs. Kansas City Royals (AL)

Of all the teams in baseball, the Philadelphia Phillies had gone the longest without winning a world championship. In 104 years, the Phillies had won just two pennants, and both times they were humiliated in the World Series. The team's 1980 pennant was won in a hair-raising NLCS against the Houston Astros, in which the final four games all went into extra innings. The Phillies had a veteran lineup that included Pete Rose, Mike Schmidt, Garry Maddox, Bake McBride, Larry Bowa, Manny Trillo, and Bob Boone. Steve Carlton won 24 games to lead a paper-thin pitching staff that relied heavily on the relief work of veterans Tug McGraw and Ron Reed. The Royals, after years of postseason frustration at the hands of the Yankees, finally made it to the World Series. Their hitting star, George Brett, had flirted with a .400 average throughout the season before ending up at .390. He also hit the homer that finally got the Royals past the Yankees in the ALCS. Brett was accompanied by a group of terrific hitters, including Amos Otis, Hal McRae, and

Willie Wilson. The Kansas City pitching staff included 20-game winner Dennis Leonard, veteran Larry Gura, Rich Gale, and submarine-baller Dan Quisenberry, who had blossomed into the league's top reliever.

The Phillies survived a pair of homers by first baseman Willie Aikens in Game One to win 7-6 behind rookie Bob Walk and McGraw. They took Game Two with another comeback win, 6-4. The series moved to Kansas City, where the teams engaged in a thrilling seesaw battle that was decided by an Aikens single in the bottom of the 10th inning. Aikens continued to torture the Phillies in Game Four with two more home runs in a 5-3 Royals victory that tied the series.

Schmidt's two-run home run gave Philadelphia an early lead in Game Five, but the Royals battled back and handed the ball to Quisenberry with a 3-2 lead. With a man on first in the ninth, Quisenberry faced pinch hitter Del Unser, the hero of the NLCS. He smashed the ball down the first-base line for a run-scoring double, then scored the go-ahead run when Trillo grounded a ball off the reliever's leg. Had any of Philadelphia's three hits gone an inch or two the other way, the Royals would have won. Instead, it was the Phillies who enjoyed the 3 games to 2 lead. Game Six began as a Carlton masterpiece and ended as a Mc-Graw nail-biter. McGraw needed to work out of two bases-loaded jams to preserve the 4-1 win and give the Phillies their first championship.

Phillies 4
Best Players: Steve Carlton
              (2-0, 2.40 ERA);
              Mike Schmidt
              (.381 BA, 7 RBIs)
Royals 2
Best Player: Willie Aikens
              (4 HR, 8 RBIs)

Mike Schmidt is on top of the world after his Phillies end their 104-year championship drought.

1981
Los Angeles Dodgers (NL)
vs. New York Yankees (AL)

Thanks to a midseason strike, baseball lost more than 50 games in 1981. It gained a preview of its future, however, when the leagues added a second round of playoffs, in which the first-half division winners played the second-half division winners. This left the team with the best record in baseball, the Cincinnati Reds, completely out of the postseason, while allowing the Yankees and Dodgers (who had miserable second halves) to make the playoffs. When the dust settled, it was Los Angeles and New York for the third time in five years.

The Yankees were a team in some disarray. After Thurman Munson's death in a 1979 plane crash and the unexpected loss to the Royals in the 1980 ALCS, George Steinbrenner had become even less patient with his personnel and managers. With a month to go, he fired Gene Michael and re-hired Bob Lemon, who had guided the 1978 club to the championship. Lemon had just two reliable hitters, Jerry Mumphrey and celebrated free agent Dave Winfield. Lemon's pitching looked a little better, with Ron Guidry, Tommy John, rookie Dave Righetti, and closer Goose Gossage turning in solid years. The Yanks beat the Brewers and A's in the playoffs to win the pennant, while the Dodgers had to get past the Astros and Expos in two grueling series. Los Angeles had a dominant pitching staff, with Burt Hooton, Jerry Reuss, and Fernando Valenzuela posting ERAs under 2.50. Valenzuela was the story of the year, throwing eight shutouts at the age of 20 and packing ballparks wherever he pitched. The Garvey-Lopes-Russell-Cey infield was still

intact, and Dusty Baker had a great year. The biggest difference in the Dodgers, however, was rookie Pedro Guerrero, who hit everything hard all year.

The Yankees took the lead in Game One on a three-run blast by Bob Watson in the first inning. They went on to win 5-3, then captured Game Two on a 3-0 shutout by John and Gossage. With the series moving to Los Angeles, the Dodgers needed a big performance out of Valenzuela. Visions of a Yankee sweep haunted L.A. fans when Valenzuela gave up homers to Watson and Rick Cerone, but he settled down, and the Dodgers came back to win 5-4. They tied the series the next day, when reliever Steve Howe came in and quelled a New York comeback to preserve an 8-7 win.

Game Five featured a brilliant pitching duel between Guidry and Reuss. Trailing 1-0 in the seventh, the Dodgers took the lead when Guerrero and Yeager homered on successive pitches. The sudden loss brought Steinbrenner down to the locker room, where he unleashed a tirade and singled out some of his best players for their poor performances—including Winfield, who managed just one hit in the entire series. Their confidence shot, the team returned to Yankee Stadium, where the Dodgers administered a 9-2 beating to end the series.

Dodgers 4
Best Players: Pedro Guerrero (.333 BA, 7 RBIs); Ron Cey (.350 BA, 6 RBIs)
Yankees 2
Best Player: Tommy John (0.69 ERA in 2 starts)

1982
St. Louis Cardinals (NL) vs. Milwaukee Brewers (AL)

On two incredible days in December 1980, manager Whitey Herzog of the St. Louis Cardinals acquired ace closers Rollie Fingers and Bruce Sutter in blockbuster deals. A few days later, he traded Fingers, catcher Ted Simmons, and pitcher Pete Vukovich to the Brewers. In 1982, these three would boost Milwaukee to the World Series. Simmons beefed up an offense that already featured Robin Yount, Paul Molitor, Ben Oglivie, and Gorman Thomas. Vukovich became the big winner on a staff that included Mike Caldwell, Moose Haas, and late-season pickup Don Sutton. As luck would have it, their foes in the series were Herzog's Cardinals.

The Cards were built around speed and defense. Ozzie Smith, acquired from the Padres for Garry Templeton, had come into his own as a shortstop, while rightfielder George Hendrick and first baseman Keith Hernandez were excellent fielders and clutch hitters. Besides the fleet-footed Smith, speed was supplied by former Phillie Lonnie Smith and rookie Willie McGee. Darrell Porter, who had starred for Herzog in Kansas City, was signed during that same amazing week in 1980 to handle the team's catching. Starters Bob Forsch, John Stuper, and Joaquin Andujar were good enough to hand games over to St. Louis's superb bullpen. The difference in this series was expected to be relief pitching. Sutter was coming off a 36-save season; Fingers was out with an injury, leaving Milwaukee with curve baller Bob McClure to finish its games.

In this war of speed versus power, power prevailed—but not always as antici-

pated. The Brewers swamped the Cardinals in Game One 10-0 on a three-hitter by Caldwell. Game Two went to St. Louis, when Porter doubled to tie the score 4-4 in the sixth and reliever Pete Ladd walked home the deciding run two innings later. Head-

Joaquin Andujar kicks and fires. He pitched a pair of beauties against the hard-hitting Brewers in the 1982 World Series.

liners Andujar and Vukovich hooked up for Game Three, but the man who made headlines was McGee. He snuffed out Milwaukee rallies with great catches in the first and last innings and clouted a pair of homers in an exciting 6-2 win. The Brewers' bats came back in Game Four, as Milwaukee scored six two-out runs in the seventh inning to cap a 7-5 comeback win and knot the series. Yount's four hits unknotted the series the next day, as Caldwell won again, 6-4.

Needing two wins at home to win the championship, the Cardinals took a page out of the Brewers' book in Game Six with a 13-1 victory. In Game Seven, Milwaukee grabbed a 3-1 lead against Andujar. Once again the St. Louis batters made the difference, however, pounding Vukovich and three relievers for 15 hits in a 6-3 comeback victory.

> **Cardinals 4**
> Best Players: Joaquin Andujar
> (2-0, 1.35 ERA);
> Bruce Sutter (1-0, 2 SV)
>
> **Brewers 3**
> Best Player: Mike Caldwell
> (2-0, 2.04 ERA)

1983
Philadelphia Phillies (NL) vs. Baltimore Orioles (AL)

In World Series play, experience often wins out over youth. This was what the Phillies were hoping for. The team was led by a group of players in their 30s and 40s, including Mike Schmidt, Steve Carlton, Pete Rose, Joe Morgan, Garry Maddox, and Tony Perez. Sportswriters, playing off the nickname of the famous 1950 club, called them the "Wheeze Kids." Philadelphia's strength was its bullpen. Willie Hernandez, Al Holland, and Ron Reed held whatever leads the starting staff could give them, which was enough to win the division and the pennant. The Orioles had a nucleus of excellent young players in Cal Ripken, Eddie Murray, and Mike Boddicker, as well as an outfield that included six players whom manager Joe Altobelli could shift back and forth to get the matchups he wanted in key situations. The experts were betting that Boddicker, Storm Davis, Scott McGregor, and Mike Flanagan would stifle the Philly hitting attack, which was the fifth-worst in the majors.

The experts had not counted on 19-game winner John Denny's opening-game five-hit gem, which gave the Phillies a 2-1 victory. The Philly bats produced just one run in Game Two, however, as Boddicker won 4-1. Carlton pitched well when the series moved to Philadelphia, but an error by shortstop Ivan DeJesus cost him a win, and the Orioles prevailed 3-2. Veteran Jim Palmer got the victory in relief, making it a record 17 years between his first and last World Series triumphs.

Game Four featured Denny, going again on three days' rest, and Davis, who was 13-7 in his first year as a starter. The Phillies took a 3-2 lead in the fifth on hits by Denny and Rose, but Baltimore's awesome bench came into play in the sixth. Three pinch hitters helped the Orioles retake the lead, and they went on to win 5-3. As predicted, the Baltimore arms beat the Philadelphia bats. Relievers Sammy Stewart and Tippy Martinez were sensational in Games Three and Four, but their services were not required in Game Five, as McGregor blanked the Phillies 5-0 to wrap up the series.

> **Orioles 4**
> Best Players: Rick Dempsey
> (.385 BA, 5 XBH);
> Tippy Martinez (key
> saves in Games 3 and 4)
> **Phillies 1**
> Best Player: Joe Morgan (2 HR, 1 SB)

1984
San Diego Padres (NL) vs. Detroit Tigers (AL)

The Tigers roared to the pennant by 15 games in 1984 with a team of steady, solid veterans, including All-Stars Alan Trammell, Lou Whitaker, Chet Lemon, Lance Parrish, and Kirk Gibson. The pitching staff was led by Jack Morris, with starters Dan Petry and Milt Wilcox chipping in 35 wins. The Tiger bullpen was one of the best ever, with Willie Hernandez and Aurelio "Señor Smoke" Lopez. These two teamed up for 19 victories and 46 saves.

By contrast, the Padres were made up of a few stars and a lot of role players. Tony Gwynn, who won his first batting title in 1984, led a roster that included former World Series heroes Steve Garvey, Goose Gossage, and Graig Nettles. The Padres' pitching was only so-so, with starters Eric Show, Ed Whitson, and Mark Thurmond. No one expected the Padres to make it to the Fall Classic. They won in a weak division and then fell behind the Cubs 2 games to 0 in the NLCS before taking three straight to win the pennant. San Diego's Dick Williams and Detroit's Sparky Anderson

each joined the select club of managers to win pennants in both the AL and the NL. One would become the first ever to win championships for both leagues.

The Tigers won the opener 3-2 on a two-run homer by outfielder Larry Herndon, a brilliant fielding play by Gibson, and a complete game by Morris. The Padres appeared beaten in Game Two when Detroit knocked Whitson out in the first inning. But Andy Hawkins and Craig Lefferts shut the Tigers out the rest of the way, and Kurt Bevacqua hit a three-run homer off Petry to win it 5-3.

With Games Three through Five scheduled for Detroit, the Padres had to win at least once in Tiger Stadium to bring the series back home. They were unable to accomplish this task, as their opponents controlled the rest of the action. The Tigers scored early in all three games and held on to win each time. Wilcox and Hernandez combined for a 5-2 win in Game Three. Morris went the distance again in Game Four and won 4-2 with help from Trammell, who homered twice. In Game Five, Gibson broke a 3-3 tie when he scored from third on a pop fly to the second baseman, then busted the game open in the eighth with an upper-deck homer off Gossage. Detroit came out with an 8-4 win.

> **Tigers 4**
> Best Players: Jack Morris (2-0, 2 CG);
> Kirk Gibson (7 RBIs,
> great defense)
> **Padres 1**
> Best Player: Kurt Bevacqua
> (.412 BA, H in
> every game)

1985
St. Louis Cardinals (NL)
vs. Kansas City Royals (AL)

In 1985, the League Championship Series format was extended from a best-of-five format to a best-of-seven. That suited the Royals just fine, since they dropped three of the first four games to the Toronto Blue Jays in the ALCS before rallying to capture the pennant. Kansas City, led again by George Brett, featured a young pitching staff that starred Danny Jackson, Mark Gubicza, Charlie Liebrandt, and Bret Saberhagen, who went 20-6 at the age of 21. Veteran Dan Quisenberry was still getting the job done in the bullpen, with 8 wins and 37 saves.

The Cardinals were built on raw speed. During the regular season, Rookie Vince Coleman swiped 110 bases, and Willie McGee—who won the batting title—chipped in 56. Hitting behind these two was second baseman Tom Herr, who knocked in 110 runs, and Jack Clark, who reached the postseason for the first time after playing seven seasons with the Giants. The St. Louis mound corps was anchored by 21-game winners John Tudor and Joaquin Andujar, as well as rookie Todd Worrell, who took over as closer in August and did a great job. The Cards were favored to win the series, even without the services of Coleman, who had been injured in the NLCS and was not available.

The Cardinals won the first two games in Kansas City and put the Royals in an immediate hole. Tudor pitched well in a 3-1 win in the opener. In Game Two, St. Louis turned a 2-0 ninth-inning deficit into a 4-2 comeback victory with a winning effort against Kansas City pitchers Liebrandt and

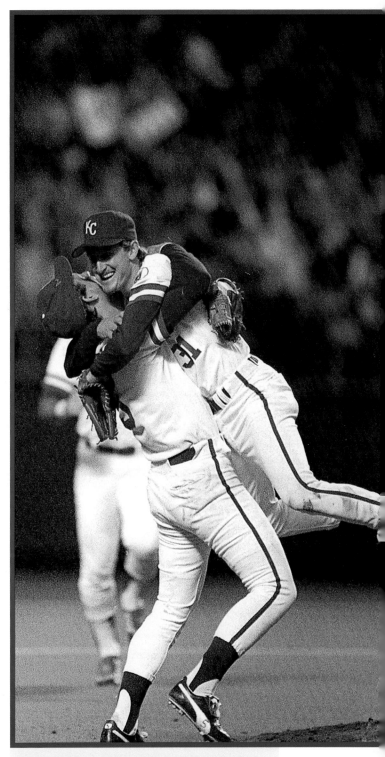

George Brett hugs Bret Saberhagen after the final out of his Game Seven win. The Royals came back from a 3-games-to-1 deficit.

BEST COMEBACK:
NEW YORK METS, 1986

Howard Johnson is the first to greet Ray Knight as he scores the winning run in Game Six of the 1986 World Series. He came home on Bill Buckner's error.

You know you have made a great comeback when the players in the other dugout begin to climb the steps to celebrate a championship, then have to quickly slink back to the bench. The Boston Red Sox had watched the California Angels do just that in the 1986 ALCS when pitcher Donnie Moore gave up a ninth-inning homer to Dave Henderson, thus denying the Angels a chance to go to the World Series. Boston went on to win that game and the next two. The Angels never knew what hit them.

In Game Six of the 1986 World Series, the tables were turned on the Red Sox. After losing the first two games at home, the New York Mets went up to Fenway Park and won two of three to bring the series back to Shea Stadium. The Red Sox, hoping to close the Mets out and avoid a seventh game, nursed a 3-2 lead into the bottom of the eighth. Two mishandled bunts gave the Mets the run they needed, and the game went into extra innings. In the top of the tenth, Boston fashioned a two-run lead on a solo homer by Dave Henderson, along with hits by Wade Boggs and Marty Barrett. Down two runs with just three outs to go, the never-say-die Mets finally looked beaten. Twenty-four-year-old Calvin Schiraldi, a former Met, retired the first two batters, Wally Backman and Keith Hernandez. Hernandez retired to the clubhouse and lit up a cigarette, figuring his team was finished. There he encountered Kevin Mitchell, who was stripping off his uniform and getting ready to shower. Out on the field, the Shea Stadium scoreboard flashed "Congratulations Red Sox" as Gary Carter settled into the batter's box.

A team does not get any closer to losing than this.

Carter worked Schiraldi like an old pro, waiting for a pitch he liked and then rapping a two-strike single. Mitchell, who was quickly summoned from the clubhouse, was sent in to pinch-hit. He had re-dressed so hastily that he was wearing nothing under his uniform. Mitchell reached out and poked a single to right. Next, Ray Knight got just enough of a Schiraldi fastball to push it up the middle and into centerfield. The hit scored Carter to make the score 5-4. Fearing Schiraldi was unraveling, Boston manager John McNamara brought in veteran righty Bob Stanley. He threw two beautiful pitches to Mookie Wilson, who fouled them both away. Stanley's third pitch, however, sailed a foot inside. Wilson jumped backward, catcher Rich Gedman failed to glove it, and Mitchell scampered in from third base with the tying run.

With the Mets suddenly and unbelievably back in the ball game, Stanley's job was to end the damage there. This he did, getting Wilson to hit a slow chopper down the first-base line. Bill Buckner, playing behind the bag, positioned himself in front of the grounder and glanced momentarily to see where Wilson was. In that instant, the ball took a funny hop, went through Buckner's legs, and continued into the outfield. Knight, holding his head in disbelief, scored all the way from second base to win the game. The Mets mounted another spirited comeback the next evening to snatch the championship from the Red Sox.

Quisenberry. Second baseman Frank White homered and doubled, and Saberhagen shut down the Cards to capture Game Three, but Tudor turned in another fine performance the next evening to earn a 3-0 shutout for St. Louis.

Down 3 games to 1, the Royals had to win the final contest in St. Louis in order to earn a trip back home. This they accomplished by a score of 6-1 with a clutch game by Jackson, who went all the way. Game Six was a nail-biter, with the Cardinals scratching out a run against Liebrandt to enter the bottom of the ninth needing just three outs to capture the championship. Worrell got pinch hitter Jorge Orta to tap to Clark at first base, but Worrell was late in covering. Worrell took Clark's throw on the run and appeared to touch the base with his foot before Orta arrived, but umpire Don Denkinger signaled Orta safe. Two more fielding mistakes loaded the bases with Royals, and pinch hitter Dane Iorg—a hitting star for the Cards in 1982—beat his old buddies with a broken-bat single for a 2-1. The series was deadlocked at 3 games to 3.

The shell-shocked Cardinals blew up in Game Seven, with Andujar getting thrown out of the game and the St. Louis hitters helpless against Saberhagen, who won 11-0.

> **Royals 4**
> Best Players: Bret Saberhagen
> (2-0, 1 ER);
> Willie Wilson
> (.367, 3 SB)
> **Cardinals 3**
> Best Player: John Tudor (2-0)

1986
New York Mets (NL) vs. Boston Red Sox (AL)

After several horrible seasons following the 1977 trade of Tom Seaver, the Mets began to rebuild themselves into a powerhouse club. For veteran leadership, the Mets acquired Keith Hernandez, Gary Carter, and Ray Knight and hired former Oriole Davey Johnson to manage. The team's young talent included pitchers Sid Fernandez, Ron Darling, Rick Aguilera, Roger McDowell, and Dwight Gooden, as well as outfielders Darryl Strawberry, Len Dykstra, and Kevin Mitchell. After second-place finishes in 1984 and 1985, the Mets won their division by 21.5 games and defeated Houston in an exciting NLCS. The Red Sox reached the World Series on the arm of the amazing Roger Clemens, who went 24-4 and led the AL in ERA. The "Rocket" was supported by the bats of Wade Boggs, Jim Rice, Dwight Evans, and Dave Henderson, who homered in the ALCS when Boston was a strike away from defeat. Veterans Bill Buckner, Marty Barrett, Rich Gedman, Don Baylor, Bruce Hurst, and Bob Stanley rounded out a solid team.

The Red Sox got off to a roaring start, taking the first two games in Shea Stadium. Game One featured a pitching battle between lefty Bruce Hurst and Darling. Boston prevailed 1-0 on a walk, a wild pitch, and an error. In Game Two, the Mets' pitching came unglued. Boston amassed 18 hits on its way to a 9-3 win and a commanding 2 games to 0 series lead as the teams headed up to Boston. No team had ever lost the World Series after winning the first two games in the enemy's ballpark.

The Fenway faithful watched in dismay

as the Red Sox proceeded to blow this advantage, losing Game Three 7-1 and Game Four 6-2. Hurst dominated the Mets again in Game Five, winning 4-2 and leaving the Red Sox one win shy of their first world title in 68 years. Game Six, back in New York, was a tense affair that went into extra innings tied 3-3. In the top of the tenth, Henderson homered, and two more hits brought in a second Boston run to make the score 5-3. In the bottom of the inning, Calvin Schiraldi got the first two Mets to fly out, but he ran into trouble when he yielded a run on three singles. With a disheartened crowd suddenly ecstatic, the Mets tied the score on a wild pitch by Stanley. Mookie Wilson, batting with two strikes, then grounded a ball to first baseman Bill Buckner. Buckner took his eye off the ball to glance at the speedy Wilson. The ball skipped through his legs, and Knight scored the winning run. The following evening, Hurst blew a 3-0 lead, and the Boston bullpen gave up five more runs to lose 8-5.

> **Mets 4**
> Best Players: Ray Knight (.391 BA);
> Ron Darling (3 quality
> starts, 1.53 ERA)
> **Red Sox 3**
> Best Player: Bruce Hurst
> (2-0, 1.96 ERA)

1987
St. Louis Cardinals (NL) vs. Minnesota Twins (AL)

When the season began, no one picked the Twins and Cardinals to be the last two teams standing. Both clubs were good but not great. As the season progressed, however, each club won the games it had to, when it had to. St. Louis edged the Mets in the NL East on huge seasons from Vince Coleman, Ozzie Smith, Jack Clark, and Willie McGee. An injury-riddled pitching staff limped into the postseason with Danny Cox and John Tudor as its only dependable starters, but Todd Worrell was great all year. Down 3 games to 2 to the Giants in the playoffs, the Cards responded with two shutouts to win the pennant. The Twins were returning to the postseason for the first time since 1970, but with a team built to win in their cozy domed ballpark. Top hitters Kirby Puckett, Kent Hrbek, Tom Brunansky, and Gary Gaetti helped Minnesota build baseball's best home record. The team's pitching centered on starters Frank Viola and Bert Blyleven (a member of the Twins' last division winner) and closer Jeff Reardon. Expected to lose to the Tigers in the ALCS, Minnesota upset Detroit 4 games to 1.

In the first World Series game ever played indoors, the Twins torched Joe Magrane and Bob Forsch for seven runs in the fourth inning on their way to a 10-1 victory. The fourth inning was good to Minnesota again in Game Two. This time the Twins lit up Cox and reliever Lee Tunnell for six runs and went on to win 8-4. The Cardinals restored order to the series when it moved to St. Louis. A seventh-inning rally gave Tudor a 3-1 win in Game Three, while Game Four saw the Cards make the fourth inning their own, with six runs en route to a 7-2 triumph. The Cardinals also took Game Five behind a superb effort by Cox, who won 4-2.

Game Six, back in the Metrodome, was played to constant and sometimes deafening crowd noise. Tudor struggled mightily but managed to wriggle out of trouble after yielding two first-inning runs. Meanwhile, the Cardinals scored five times off Les Straker and Dan Schatzeder. Designated hitter Don Baylor got the Twins back in the game with a three-run homer in the fifth, and Hrbek put it away with a grand slam in the sixth to give Minnesota an 11-5 win and force a seventh game. The finale pitted Magrane against Viola. St. Louis took a 2-0 lead, but the Twins chipped away for four single runs. Viola and Reardon closed out a 4-2 win that gave Minnesota its first baseball championship since the franchise moved from Washington, D.C., 26 years earlier.

Twins 4
  Best Players: Frank Viola (2 W);
                 Kirby Puckett
                 (6 H in Games
                 6 and 7)
Cardinals 3
  Best Player: Vince Coleman
                 (5 SB in 3 St. Louis W)

1988
Los Angeles Dodgers (NL)
vs. Oakland A's (AL)

It had been years since the American League had a true powerhouse club, but the Oakland A's had all the earmarks of a dynasty in the making. Manager Tony La Russa had a couple of great young hitters in Jose Canseco and Mark McGwire, as well as a pitching staff that featured veterans Dave Stewart, Bob Welch, Storm Davis, and reliever Dennis Eckersley, who saved 45 games. The rest of the A's were above-

average support players who understood their jobs and did them well. The Dodgers, on the other hand, were a weird collection of eccentrics, castoffs, and players on the rebound who came together under manager Tom Lasorda and former Tiger Kirk Gibson. No Dodger hit more than 25 homers or batted .300, and the team RBI leader was outfielder Mike Marshall, with 82. The pitching staff was led by Orel Hershiser, who went 23-8 and ended the season with a mind-boggling six straight shutouts. In the NLCS, the Dodgers shocked the powerful Mets to earn a shot at the mighty A's, but they lost their MVP, Kirk Gibson, to a crippling knee injury.

Fans quickly got the sense that this World Series would not play out the way everyone was predicting. Mickey Hatcher, who hit just one homer during the season, lined a first-inning pitch by Stewart over the leftfield wall for a 2-0 lead. A few minutes later, Canseco blasted a Tim Belcher delivery out of Dodger Stadium with the bases loaded for a 4-2 lead. Down 4-3 with two out and one man on in the ninth, the Dodgers sent Gibson limping to the plate. Eckersley got two quick strikes, then tried to sneak a "backdoor slider" past him. Gibson, who was looking for the pitch, stroked it into the rightfield bleachers and hobbled around the bases in triumph. The A's had to face the red-hot Hershiser in Game Two. He not only shut them out 6-0 on three hits, but also ignited the decisive five-run third inning with a single off Davis.

Oakland pulled out Game Three 2-1 on a McGwire home run in the bottom of the ninth, but the Dodgers scored a one-run victory the next evening against Stewart, 4-3. Any thoughts the A's had of coming back in this series probably ended at the start of Game Five, when Hatcher drilled another two-run homer in the first inning. Mike Davis, who had just two regular-season round-trippers, put the game away with a two-run blast in the fourth. Hershiser went the distance again on a four-hitter, winning 5-2 to give the Dodgers their seventh world championship in 33 seasons.

Dodgers 4
Best Players: Orel Hershiser (2-0, 1.00 ERA); Mickey Hatcher (.368 BA, 2 HR)

A's 1
Best Player: Terry Steinbach (.364 BA)

Kirk Gibson raises the only limb that doesn't hurt as he hobbles triumphantly around the bases. His pinch-hit home run against Dennis Eckersley turned the tide of the 1988 World Series.

1989
San Francisco Giants (NL)
vs. Oakland A's (AL)

The Oakland offense never really recovered from its dismal showing in the 1988 World Series. Mark McGwire hit .231, Dave Henderson struck out 131 times, and Jose Canseco missed half the year with injuries and hit only 17 home runs. The A's won their division thanks to great pitching by Dave Stewart, Mike Moore, Storm Davis, Bob Welch—who won a total of 76 games—and Dennis Eckersley, who saved 33 games and had a 1.56 ERA. The offense was led by third baseman Carney Lansford, who hit .336 and stole 37 bases, and former A's star Rickey Henderson, who was reacquired from the floundering Yankees at midseason and led the AL in walks, runs,

Oakland closer Dennis Eckersley helps umpire Al Clark call the final out of the 1989 World Series.

and steals. The Giants were led by super-charged slugger Will Clark and Kevin Mitchell, who blossomed into the league's top home-run hitter after leaving the Mets. The San Francisco offense also got a boost from speedy Brett Butler and young Matt Williams, who clubbed 18 home runs in limited regular-season action. The veteran pitching staff was anchored by 40-year-old Rick Reuschel.

Oakland struck early and often in this series, starting in Game One. The A's staked Stewart to a quick 3-0 lead and added single runs on homers by Dave Parker and Walt Weiss. Stewart went all the way on a five-hit shutout. Game Two was close for a few innings, but Terry Steinbach's three-run homer in the fourth sunk the Giants, who lost 5-1 to Mike Moore.

Game Three, across the bay in San Francisco, was delayed for ten days by the devastating earthquake that rocked Northern California. When play resumed, Stewart took the mound again and cruised to a 13-7 win that featured five Oakland home runs. The A's, who never trailed in the series for even a single inning, jumped out to a 8-0 lead in Game Four, and Moore let the bullpen finish off a 9-6 win. Never before had one team so decisively swept another in World Series play.

A's 4
Best Players: Dave Stewart
(2-0, 1.69 ERA);
Rickey Henderson
(.474 BA)
Giants 0
Best Player: Kevin Mitchell
(.294 BA, 1 HR)

THE 1990s

1990
Cincinnati Reds (NL)
vs. Oakland A's (AL)

The Oakland A's were the talk of the American League once again. Mark McGwire and Jose Canseco each topped 35 homers and 100 RBIs. Rickey Henderson led the league in runs and stolen bases, and Bob Welch and Dave Stewart won almost 50 games between them. Dennis Eckersley had his greatest year, with 48 saves and a 0.81 ERA.

The talk of the National League was the "Nasty Boys," a trio of snarling, hard-throwing relievers who occupied the Cincinnati bullpen. Manager Lou Piniella looked for six innings out of his starters (Jose Rijo, Danny Jackson, and Tom Browning) and then handed the ball to Norm Charlton, Rob Dibble, and Randy Myers. Thanks to his pitchers—and solid years from Barry Larkin, Chris Sabo, Eric Davis, and Billy Hatcher—Piniella took the same team that had finished 12 games under .500 in 1989 and won the NL pennant.

The series opener, in Cincinnati, treated fans to the rare sight of Stewart getting his rear end kicked in a 7-0 win for the Reds. Game Two suddenly became a big one for the A's, who started Welch, their 27-game winner. The Reds reached him for two runs in the first, but he settled down and took a 4-3 lead into the eighth. Hatcher, who had yet to be retired by the A's in the series, reached base a record seventh time in a row with a line drive to rightfield, which Canseco misplayed into a triple. Hatcher scored the tying run a few moments later on a groundout. In the tenth inning, the A's brought Eckersley into the game in a rare nonsave situation. After allowing an infield hit and a solid single to Sabo, Eck got catcher Joe Oliver to bounce to Carney Lansford. Somehow the ball eluded the third baseman, and the Reds scored the winning run.

Things got even weirder for the A's in Game Three. Up 2-1 in the third inning, the sure-handed McGwire bobbled an easy grounder, and the pitching staff suddenly self-destructed. By the time the third out was recorded, Cincinnati had scored seven times, and they went on to win 8-3. Stewart came back in Game Four and pitched wonderfully, but he lost a 2-1 game to Rijo when his eighth-inning throwing error allowed the Reds to score the winning run. As World Series sweeps go, it was one of the most remarkable ever.

Fireballer Jose Rijo waves to friends and family after completing the unlikeliest of sweeps against the powerhouse Oakland A's.

Reds 4
Best Players: Jose Rijo (2-0, 0.59 ERA);
Billy Hatcher (.750 BA)

A's 0
Best Player: Rickey Henderson (.333 BA)

1991
Atlanta Braves (NL) vs. Minnesota Twins (AL)

In the age of free agents, it was believed, a team could go from "worst to first" simply by purchasing the players it needed. This had yet to happen, and free agency was now almost 15 years old. The Braves and Twins finally broke through in 1991. Last in their respective divisions in 1990, these teams did indeed win their respective pennants. However, they did so with just one key free-agent signing with each. The Twins got pitcher Jack Morris, who won 18 games and provided strong leadership. It was the hurling of young starters Scott Erickson and Kevin Tapani that put Minnesota over the top. Left over from the 1987 team were Kirby Puckett, Dan Gladden, and Kent Hrbek. Rookie Chuck Knoblauch and newcomers Chili Davis and Shane Mack bolstered the offense, while Rick Aguilera, converted to a relief role, picked up 42 saves.

The Braves' major free-agent addition was former Cardinal Terry Pendleton, who led the league with a .319 average and played great defense at third base. But it was the maturing of young pitchers John Smoltz, Tom Glavine, and Steve Avery—along with a nice comeback year from veteran Charlie Liebrandt—that enabled Atlanta to edge the Los Angeles Dodgers in the NL West. Dave Justice, the rookie sensation of 1990, battled a sore back to put up good numbers; Ron Gant had a 30-30 year; and Otis Nixon stole 72 bases after coming to Atlanta in an April 1 trade. The Braves stunned the Pirates in the NLCS, winning Games Six and Seven on shutouts.

No one knew quite what to expect from the Twins and Braves. Would they play like last-place teams or first-place teams? Game One held no answers. The Twins scored five times on homers by Hrbek and shortstop Greg Gagne, while Morris limited the Braves to two runs in an easy win. Things heated up in Game Two, however, when Glavine and Tapani kept the score at 2-2 for seven innings. The game was decided on an eighth-inning homer by Minnesota utility man Scott Leius, and Aguilera closed out

BEST CLUTCH PERFORMANCE:
JACK MORRIS AND KIRBY PUCKETT, 1991

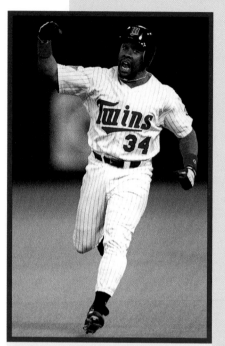

Kirby Puckett raises a fist in victory as he rounds the bases after his Game Six home run. Puckett and pitcher Jack Morris came up big when the Twins needed them most.

Clutch plays win World Series. When the Minnesota Twins fell behind the Atlanta Braves 3 games to 2 in the 1991 World Series, they knew they needed someone to step up and take over. They never expected two players to answer the call. Before Game Six, centerfielder Kirby Puckett—in the midst of a lackluster series—started to get things going in the clubhouse. "Jump on board, boys," he said, "I'm going to carry us tonight. Just back me up a little and I'll take us to Game Seven!"

In the third inning, with a man on first base and the score tied 2-2, Atlanta's Ron Gant nailed a pitch on a line toward the left-centerfield wall. Puckett raced over, found the wall, leaped high, and grabbed the ball off the top of the glass for a spectacular catch. He had already knocked in and scored a run, and in the bottom of the fourth he broke the deadlock with his second hit of the game. The Braves tied the score at 3-3 in the seventh, and the game went into extra innings.

Atlanta reliever Alejandro Pena blew the Twins away in the ninth and tenth innings, but Carl Willis and Rick Aguilera of the Twins held the Braves scoreless right through the 11th. As the Twins came off the field and prepared to bat in the bottom of the 11th, Puckett looked over and saw Charlie Liebrandt warming up in the Braves' bullpen. Puckett had hit him well in the past. As Puckett and Chili Davis swung weighted bats waiting for the inning to begin, Puckett asked for the veteran's advice. Davis urged Puckett to lay off Liebrandt's low pitches and force him to get the ball up. "Go ahead and get this over with," Davis said.

Puckett took the first two pitches. Both were low and away, the first a ball and the second a strike. Liebrandt's third delivery was high and tight. The crafty lefty was sending a message to Puckett. He was telling him not to get too aggressive with the next pitch, which Puckett was supposed to believe would be another low fastball. Liebrandt actually hoped to get him swinging early so that he could fool him with a change-up. But Puckett knew something was up. He stayed back, waited for the pitch, and his eyes lit up when he saw the off-speed pitch coming in just where he liked it. A couple of seconds later, the ball was sailing into the leftfield stands and the crowd nearly blew the lid off the Metrodome. Minnesota was a 4-3 winner, and the Braves were forced to play a seventh game.

The starting pitcher for the Twins in Game Seven was veteran Jack Morris. The former Detroit Tiger faced young John Smoltz. Smoltz had grown up in Michigan idolizing Morris. He was thrilled when he was drafted by the Tigers in 1985, then devastated when Detroit traded him to the Braves during the 1987 season. Smoltz did his best Jack Morris imitation in this pressure-packed game, limiting the Twins to four hits and no runs through seven innings. Morris, working out of trouble a couple of times, kept the Braves off the scoreboard as well. Never before had a Game Seven remained scoreless for so long.

The Twins got a break in the eighth after Atlanta's Lonnie Smith singled off Morris. Smith took off for second on a pitch that Terry Pendleton lined to leftfield for a double. The speedy Smith should have scored easily, but Minnesota infielders Greg Gagne and Chuck Knoblauch set up for a phony relay and Smith hesitated, thinking the ball might have been caught. By the time he saw the ball rattling around the outfield, it was too late to break for home. With no one out and men on second and third, Morris took over. He got Gant to ground out, with both runners holding their bases. Then he intentionally walked Dave Justice to set up a force at every base. Keeping the ball low, Morris got Sid Bream to hit a sharp grounder to first. Kent Hrbek whipped the ball home to catcher Brian Harper. Harper stepped on the plate to retire Smith, then threw back to first to nip Bream for a double play.

The Braves pulled off a game-saving double play of their own in the bottom of the eighth, and when both teams failed to score in the ninth, a World Series seventh game went to extra innings for the first time since 1924.

While Minnesota batted in the ninth, manager Tom Kelly informed Morris that he was through for the night. Morris glared back at Kelly. Kelly got the message: There was no way Morris was leaving this game. When the Twins took the field for the tenth, he was still on the mound.

After pitching his tenth inning of shutout baseball, Morris plopped down on the bench and started wondering if the game would ever end. His spirits soared when leadoff hitter Dan Gladden blooped a hit to leftfield and legged out a double. Knoblauch bunted Gladden to third, then the Braves walked Puckett and Hrbek intentionally to set up a force at home, just as the Twins had two innings earlier. The outfield was drawn in to prevent any short hits as pinch hitter Gene Larkin came to the plate. Larkin got the job done, lifting a long fly to rightfield to win the World Series.

No pitcher had ever been asked to do as much—for so long and under such dramatic circumstances—as Morris had in Game Seven. And no one had ever taken over a game quite like Puckett had in Game Six. Together these stars brought a championship to Minnesota and, with their clutch performances, almost certainly guaranteed their future places in the Baseball Hall of Fame.

the 3-2 victory. The Braves battled back when the series shifted to Atlanta. Second baseman Mark Lemke singled home the winning run in Game Three, which was a 5-4, 11-inning triumph. Then he scored the winning run in a 3-2 Game Four victory with a triple off Mark Guthrie in the bottom of the ninth. Game Five went to Atlanta, too, but this time it was a 14-5 blowout. The Braves were up 3 games to 2.

Needing to win twice at home, the Twins fought another 11-inning battle in Game Six. Puckett was a one-man show, snatching a home run out of the stands and ending the game on a solo shot off Liebrandt. Game Seven was one of the best ever. Morris and Smoltz dominated the hitters, and both teams played dazzling defense to keep the game scoreless after nine innings. In the bottom of the tenth, Gladden turned a broken-bat hit into a double and went to third on a bunt. A few moments later, pinch hitter Gene Larkin drove home Gladden to end the series.

> **Twins 4**
> Best Players: Jack Morris
> (2-0, 1.17 ERA);
> Kirby Puckett
> (great Game 6)
> **Braves 3**
> Best Player: Mark Lemke (.417 BA)

1992
Atlanta Braves (NL) vs. Toronto Blue Jays (AL)

The Braves proved 1991 was not a fluke when they won their division easily. Their four starters turned in good seasons once again; their bench players made terrific contributions; and football star Deion Sanders finally began to fulfill his baseball potential with a .304 average and 26 stolen bases as a part-time leadoff man. The Pirates nearly beat Atlanta in the NLCS, but with two outs in the bottom of the ninth inning of Game Seven, pinch hitter Francisco Cabrera (the last man added to the postseason roster) singled home Sid Bream (the slowest runner in the league). Braves fans could have been excused for thinking destiny was on their side after that, but Toronto fans felt the same way. Since the 1980s, the Blue Jays had solid teams year after year, but something always seemed to prevent them from winning a pennant. The final piece of the puzzle for the Jays was free agent Jack Morris, hero of the 1991 World Series. He joined young Juan Guzman and veteran Jimmy Key in a rotation that was further improved by the late-season pickup of David Cone from the Mets. Tom "The Terminator" Henke handled bullpen duties with Duane Ward. Toronto's hitting attack featured All-Stars Roberto Alomar and Joe Carter, as well as 40-year-old Dave Winfield, who was returning to the World Series for the first time since going 1 for 22 with the Yankees in 1981.

A surprising three-run homer by catcher Damon Berryhill sent Morris to a 3-1 defeat in Game One, but the Jays took Game Two 5-4 behind great relief pitching and an equally surprising two-run blast by benchwarmer Ed Sprague. The Jays went home to SkyDome lucky to have a win, and they knew it. But it was skill, not luck, that won the next two games. Both were tense, one-run contests. Guzman outdueled Steve Avery, and Toronto took Game Three 3-2. Game Four saw Key beat Tom Glavine 2-1.

The supertight series finally opened up a bit in Game Five, as the Braves pounded out 13 hits against five Toronto pitchers for an easy 7-2 win. Game Six, in Atlanta, was an epic battle. The Jays took a 2-1 lead into the ninth but could not hold it, and the game went into extra innings. In the top of the 11th, Winfield came up with two men on base. In 43 previous World Series at bats, he had never managed more than a single. This time he lashed a Charlie Liebrandt delivery down the third-base line to give Toronto a 4-2 lead. Atlanta mounted a furious charge in the bottom half of the inning but came up a run short. Winfield had his moment of glory, and Canada had its first baseball championship. Once again, the Braves were left to wonder "What if?" after four excruciating losses.

Blue Jays 4
Best Players: Pat Borders (.450 BA);
David Wells
(0 ER in 4 relief
appearances)
Braves 2
Best Player: Deion Sanders
(.533 BA, 5 SB)

1993
Philadelphia Phillies (NL) vs. Toronto Blue Jays (AL)

The Philadelphia Phillies became the third team in three seasons to go from worst to first, as they rose from the cellar of the NL's Eastern Division in 1992 to edge the fast-improving Expos in 1993. The Phillies looked like a collection of spare parts in April, but by October they were a tough

team. Hitting stars Dave Hollins, Darren Daulton, John Kruk, and Lenny Dykstra were as hard-nosed as players come, and Philadelphia also got major years out of minor players Kevin Stocker, Pete Incaviglia, Wes Chamberlain, and Mariano Duncan. The pitching staff was thin, with Curt Schilling and Terry Mulholland as the only reliable starters. Erratic Mitch "Wild Thing" Williams saved 43 games, but few of those saves came easily.

The Blue Jays seemed to hold all the cards when the World Series started. The defending champs were without David Cone, but they had added Dave Stewart. Jack Morris had a bad elbow, but young Pat Hentgen had blossomed into a 19-game winner. And Juan Guzman continued to win despite giving up a pile of hits and walks. The Toronto offense improved with trades for Paul Molitor, Rickey Henderson, and Tony Fernandez, and first baseman John Olerud led the AL with a .363 average.

It became obvious right away that this would be a hitter's series. In the opener, Toronto won 8-5 with three runs in the bottom of the seventh. Mulholland and two relievers made Jim Eisenreich's three-run homer stand up in a 6-4 Game Two victory for Philadelphia, but the Jays struck back when the series moved to Philly. Molitor led a 13-hit attack with a homer and triple, and Hentgen pitched 6 good innings for a 10-3 win.

Game Four featured 19 runs in the first 5 innings, with the Phillies holding a less-than-commanding 12-7 lead on homers by Dykstra and Daulton. With the score 14-10 in the eighth inning, Williams was called in to close out the slugfest. Clutch hits by Henderson and Devon White gave Toronto a huge inning, and when the smoke cleared, the Jays were up by a score of 15-14. Relievers Mike Timlin and Duane Ward came in and struck out four of six Phillies to end the game. With the Philadelphia bullpen a shambles, Schilling came up big with a 2-0 shutout in Game Five. The Phillies played well in Game Six, coming from four runs down to take a 6-5 lead. Once again Williams was called on to turn out the lights in the bottom of the ninth, and once again he failed. A walk to Henderson and a single to Molitor brought veteran Joe Carter to the plate. One of baseball's best RBI men, he caught a low slider just right and sent it screaming into the stands for an 8-6 victory. The Phillies slinked off the field while the fans in SkyDome launched into a wild celebration.

Blue Jays 4
Best Players: Joe Carter
               (series-winning HR,
               8 RBIs);
               Paul Molitor
               (10 R, 500 BA)
Phillies 2
Best Player: Len Dykstra (.348, 4 HR)

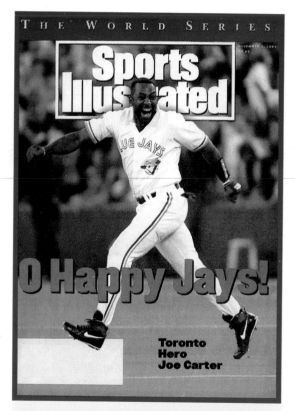

Few magazine covers have captured the joy of a winning moment as well as this 1993 issue of *Sports Illustrated.* Joe Carter starts his victorious tour around the bases after a big home run.

1994
No World Series Held

The 1994 season came to an abrupt end on August 11, when the players—unwilling to consider a salary cap proposed by the owners—chose to go on strike. When no progress was made in the negotiations, the rest of the season, including the World Series, was canceled. For the first time since 1904, there would be no postseason play.

The strike had a devastating effect on baseball. When play stopped, half of the 28 clubs were still in the running for a playoff spot, and several records were being threatened by the game's top players. Baseball fans were the ones who had to suffer through a fall without their favorite game. It took four years for the fans to "forgive" baseball and come back to the ball park. This was most evident in the TV ratings for the World Series. After 1994, the series ceased to be an important television event.

1995
Atlanta Braves (NL) vs. Cleveland Indians (AL)

After becoming baseball's beloved over-achievers in 1991, the Atlanta Braves began to acquire a reputation for choking in big games. Their loss to the Blue Jays in the 1992 World Series; their defeat by the Phillies in the 1993 NLCS; the fact that they were trailing the young, cash-poor Expos when the 1994 season was cut short—all of this made fans wonder whether Atlanta had what it took to win. The team's pitching was unimprovable. Greg Maddux, acquired in 1993, led a staff that still included John Smoltz and Tom Glavine, as well as flame-throwing reliever Mark Wohlers. The Atlanta offense had been retooled since 1991, with Dave Justice now anchoring a lineup that included sluggers Fred McGriff, Ryan Klesko, Chipper Jones, and Javier Lopez. Indeed, the 1995 Braves were one of the best teams in a generation.

The Indians had been built slowly and intelligently over the same period of time. A nucleus of young stars—all signed to long-term contracts before they were eligible for free agency—gave Cleveland a powerhouse offense. Manny Ramirez, Kenny Lofton, Albert Belle, Carlos Baerga, and Omar Vizquel helped the Tribe win 100 games in a year when only 144 games were played (due to a slow resolution of the 1994 strike). The pitching staff featured veterans Orel Hershiser, Charles Nagy, and Dennis Martinez. Although they completed a grand total of just six games, the Indians' solid middle relief and closer Jose Mesa allowed few leads to slip away.

There was a political undercurrent to this series. When these two franchises had faced each other in the 1948 World Series, no one gave their nicknames a second thought. In 1995, however, Native Americans picketed the World Series. They protested that the names "Braves" and "Indians" were de-meaning to their heritage. Although neither team changed its name, several pro and college teams in various sports did make changes over the next few years.

The Braves needed their starters to shut down the Cleveland hitting attack, and in Games One and Two they did just that. Maddux two-hit the Indians in the opener, 3-2, retiring 25 of 26 hitters during one stretch. Glavine won the next day, 4-3. Game Three, in Cleveland, was a close one. This time the Indians prevailed in 11 innings, 7-6.

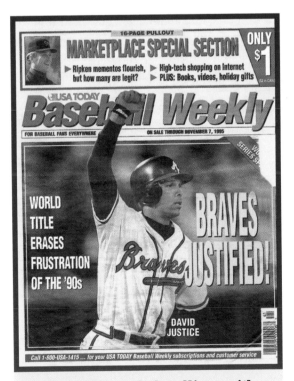

Dave Justice made headlines with his series-winning homer against the Cleveland Indians.

With a victory under their belt, the Indians sought to tie the series and swing the momentum back in their favor. They hoped to do so against Atlanta's only starter with a losing record, Steve Avery. Ken Hill, picked up in a late-season trade with the Cardinals, started for the Tribe. The two hurlers posted five scoreless innings before Klesko homered for the Braves in the sixth and Belle returned the favor for Cleveland to make it 1-1. The Braves took the lead on a Luis Polonia double in the seventh and went ahead 4-1 on a two-run single by Justice three batters later. Wohlers and Pedro Borbon, Jr., slammed the door on a 5-2 win, and the Indians found themselves in an impossible 3-1 hole. Cleveland made a gallant comeback try, beating Maddux 5-4 the next evening in Game Five. When the series returned to Atlanta, however, Glavine one-hit the Indians, and Justice—who joked that the fans might "burn our houses down" if the Braves lost—struck a blow for fire safety when he homered to wrap up the series 1-0.

> **Braves 4**
> Best Players: Tom Glavine
> (2-0, 1.29 ERA);
> Mark Wohlers
> (2 SV)
> **Indians 2**
> Best Player: Jose Mesa
> (1 W, 1 SV)

1996
Atlanta Braves (NL) vs. New York Yankees (AL)

In 1996, the Yankees returned to the World Series after making just one playoff appearance in 14 years. Under manager Joe Torre, this team of veteran role players and young stars won 92 games and then survived postseason scares against the Rangers and Orioles to win the pennant. Bernie Williams, Tino Martinez, Derek Jeter, Andy Pettitte, and Mariano Rivera gave New York a core of poised young stars, while veteran warriors Jimmy Key, David Cone, John Wetteland, Paul O'Neill, Wade Boggs, Cecil Fielder, and Darryl Strawberry rounded out a club built to win in tight situations. The Braves came into the World Series with their best club of the 1990s. Thanks to a trade for lefty Denny Neagle, the pitching was better than ever, and the team's key hitters all had fine years. Atlanta received an important injection of youth after Dave Justice suffered a season-ending shoulder injury, as rookies Jermaine Dye and Andruw Jones played their way into the everyday lineup. In the NLCS, the Cardinals shocked the Braves by taking a 3-1 series lead, but Atlanta recovered to win the final three games by a combined score of 32-1. Most picked the Braves to roll over the Yankees in the World Series.

By the third inning of Game One, Jones had already stroked a pair of home runs to become the youngest player ever to hit a World Series homer—and the first since Gene Tenace in 1972 to "leave the yard" in his first two World Series at bats. The 19-year-old's heroics highlighted a 12-1 thrashing of Pettitte, as Smoltz carried a no-hitter into the fifth inning before leaving in the seventh. Game Two featured a 4-0 shutout by Maddux that enabled the Braves to take the series home up 2 games to 0. The Yankees showed signs of waking up in Game Three. Cone pitched well and Williams hit a two-run homer to spark a 5-2 victory, but the next night the Braves jumped out to a 6-0 lead and handed the ball to Wohlers in the eighth with the score 6-3. Two hits and a botched double play brought pinch hitter Jim Leyritz to the plate with two men aboard. Wohlers, who owned a 100-mph (160-kph) fastball, decided to throw an off-speed pitch to Leyritz, and he lofted it into the leftfield seats to tie the game and breathe new life into the Bronx Bombers. They won the game two innings later 8-6 to knot the series.

The ultracompetitive Pettitte, still seething from his Game One shellacking, came back and tortured the Braves in Game Five. Smoltz was nearly as good, however, allowing just one run on an error by center-fielder Marquis Grissom. The game ended 1-0, and the Yankees, to even their own surprise, returned to the Bronx up 3 games to 2. Maddux hoped to stymie the Yanks in Game Six, but New York strung together

After a dozen years as an All-Star, Wade Boggs finally got his World Series ring in 1996. He celebrates the Yankees' victory on horseback, courtesy of a New York City cop.

four hits in the third inning and scored three runs. That was all Key needed. A timely double play cut off an Atlanta rally, and the Yankees' bullpen took over to close out the Braves 3-2 for a remarkable upset and comeback.

Yankees 4
Best Players: John Wetteland (4 SV); David Cone (big W in Game 3)
Braves 2
Best Player: John Smoltz (2 starts, 0.64 ERA)

1997
Florida Marlins (NL) vs. Cleveland Indians (AL)

The Indians were surprise pennant winners thanks to Sandy Alomar, whose homer off New York's Mariano Rivera brought Cleveland back from the dead against the Yankees in the Division Series (an extra tier of play-offs added in 1995). The Tribe then blew past the Orioles in the ALCS despite being out-hit and outpitched. Some major deals helped to reshape the Indians, with newcomers Matt Williams, Tony Fernandez, Marquis Grissom, and Dave Justice joining the Cleveland lineup. Charles Nagy and Orel Hershiser again led the pitching staff, along with young starters Jaret Wright and Chad Ogea.

Even more surprising than the AL champion Indians were the NL champion Marlins, a team that did not even exist five years earlier. Manager Jim Leyland guided this team of young prospects and high-priced free agents to a Wild Card berth, then swept the powerful Giants and defeated the mighty Braves in the playoffs. The Marlins got great pitching from veteran starters Kevin Brown and Alex Fernandez and rookie Livan Hernandez—who had defected from the Cuban national team a year earlier—pitched his heart out. The hard-throwing bullpen of Robb Nen, Jay Powell, Dennis Cook, Antonio Alfonseca, and Felix Heredia was used to perfection. Florida's key hitters included Gary Sheffield, Moises Alou, Bobby Bonilla, and Darren Daulton, as well as a speedy 21-year-old shortstop named Edgar Renteria.

Game One went to the Marlins, who got back-to-back homers from Alou and catcher Charles Johnson and great relief pitching in a 7-4 victory. The Indians pounced on Brown in Game Two, scoring six times in six innings to win 6-1, as Ogea got the decision for Cleveland. Game Three was a real slugfest, but this time the Marlins emerged as 14-11 winners. Eleven runs were scored in the ninth inning alone, as the pitching for both sides completely fell apart.

The Indians continued their lusty hitting in Game Four, while the Marlins did not. Homers by Ramirez and Williams spurred a 10-3 win. Perhaps it was the 15-degree F (-9.4-degree C) wind chill (the coldest in World Series history) that had cooled off the Florida bats. If so, they recovered in time for Game Five, which featured Alou's third home run of the series and another victory by Game One winner Hernandez, 8-7. The teams moved back to Florida for Game Six, and once again Ogea outpitched Brown, this time 4-1, to force a seventh game. Game Seven was a classic, with Cleveland taking a 2-0 lead and the Marlins tying the game in the bottom of the ninth when utilityman

The Marlins rush from their dugout to greet Craig Counsell, whose run brought a championship to Florida.

Craig Counsell tagged Mesa for a clutch sacrifice fly. Neither team scored in the 10th inning, and Powell retired the Indians in the 11th. With Nagy on the mound in relief, the Marlins loaded the bases with the help of an error by Fernandez, who earlier had driven in both of Cleveland's runs. Renteria came to the plate and slashed a "seeing-eye" hit just past Nagy and between the two middle infielders to make Florida the first Wild Card team to win a World Series.

Marlins 4
Best Players: Livan Hernandez (2 W);
Moises Alou
(3 HR, 9 RBIs)
Indians 3
Best Player: Chad Ogea
(2-0, 1.54 ERA)

1998
San Diego Padres (NL) vs. New York Yankees (AL)

A lot of fans felt the 1998 World Series was a waste of the time. The New York Yankees had just put together one of the most impressive seasons in history, winning 114 games in the regular season and taking care of the power-laden Rangers and Indians in the playoffs. Playing the Padres seemed like little more than a formality. The Yankees were a remarkably balanced ball club—a team without a true superstar, but everyone from the starters to the benchwarmers knew how to win a ball game. No Yankee hit 30 homers, and only three scored more than 100 runs. As a group, however, they were awesome. Bernie Williams won the batting title; Derek Jeter had a breakthrough year;

and newcomer Chuck Knoblauch did a good job from the leadoff spot. New York's pitching featured David Cone, Andy Pettitte, David Wells, and Orlando "El Duque" Hernandez, the older half-brother of Livan, who had escaped by boat from Cuba following the 1997 World Series. Mariano Rivera was now the team's closer, with Ramiro Mendoza and Jeff Nelson serving as setup men.

The Padres were a team that played with professionalism and won with emotion. Kevin Brown, acquired by San Diego after Marlins owner Wayne Huizenga broke up his championship team, led a staff that included starters Andy Ashby and Sterling Hitchcock, along with closer Trevor Hoffman, who saved 53 games. The offense was powered by outfielders Tony Gwynn, Steve Finley, and Greg Vaughn.

In many ways, the 1998 World Series was decided in the opener. The Yankees started their hottest hurler, Wells, against the even-hotter Brown. San Diego took a 5-2 lead on two homers by Vaughn and one by Gwynn. Brown, in apparent control of the game, allowed two base runners in the seventh. This prompted manager Bruce Bochy to lift his starter and hand the game over to his bullpen. A furious Brown watched as Knoblauch tied the score with a home run, and then Tino Martinez hit a grand slam after getting a generous call from the umpire on what looked like strike three. The 9-6 Yankee win destroyed the Padres' confidence.

Game Two saw New York score seven unanswered runs on its way to a 9-3 victory. The Yankees were pitching well, hitting well, and playing great defense. The Padres were not. Game Three, in San Diego, was close until New York third baseman Scott

Brosius hit home runs in the seventh and eighth innings to key a 5-4 win. The Yankees completed the sweep with a 3-0 shutout by Pettitte the next day. As expected, the World Series was a wipeout.

```
Yankees 4
  Best Players:  Mariano Rivera (3 SV);
                 Scott Brosius
                 (.471 BA, 6 RBIs)
Padres 0
  Best Player:   Tony Gwynn
                 (.500 BA, 3 RBIs)
```

1999
Atlanta Braves (NL) vs. New York Yankees (AL)

The Braves returned to the World Series for the fifth time in the 1990s, but for the first time they were cast in the underdog role. They were without the services of two important players: slugging first baseman Andres Galarraga (who missed the year while undergoing cancer treatment) and catcher Javier Lopez (who had injured his knee). An MVP year from Chipper Jones helped to hold off the surging Mets in the regular season, and Atlanta beat them in the NLCS. Once again, pitching was the key for the Braves. The old reliable trio of Greg Maddux, John Smoltz, and Tom Glavine got a big assist from a pair of 24-year-olds—18-game winner Kevin Millwood and John Rocker, who saved 38 games. The Yankees won "only" 98 games in 1999, but took their division easily and cruised through the playoffs. Orlando Hernandez led the staff with 17 victories, while Andy Pettitte, David Cone, and free agent Roger Clemens

chipped in 40 more. Closer Mariano Rivera was tremendous again, as was the entire New York bullpen. And the hitters all had good years, with Derek Jeter and Bernie Williams each hitting close to .350 and scoring and driving home more than 100 runs. The Braves, exhausted from their NLCS encounter with the pesky Mets, looked like easy pickings for the Yanks, who came into the World Series playing their best baseball.

The Braves knew they would go as far as their pitching took them. In Game One, Maddux took them into the eighth up 1-0. Then the Yankees scored four times, and the

Tom Glavine and his fellow Braves could not stem the Yankee tide in 1999, as the New Yorkers swept Atlanta out of the World Series.

New York bullpen cruised through the final two innings to win 4-1. Cone tossed seven innings of one-hit ball in Game Two, while his teammates drove Millwood from the game in the third inning of a 7-2 rout.

The series moved to Yankee Stadium, where the Braves made some noise with five runs in the first four innings. The Yankees used the long ball to tie the score against Glavine, who yielded homers to Chad Curtis, Tino Martinez, and Chuck Knoblauch. In the bottom of the tenth inning, Curtis clouted his second home run of the game, against reliever Mike Remlinger, to give New York a 6-5 win and a 3 games to 0 series lead. It was all over 24 hours later, after the Yankees put up three early runs against Smoltz and Clemens threw well in a 4-1 victory. Although the Braves made a couple of games close, a second straight Yankee championship never really seemed in doubt.

Yankees 4
Best Players: Mariano Rivera
(1 W, 2 SV);
Chuck Knoblauch
(.313 BA, 5 R)
Braves 0
Best Player: Bret Boone (.538 BA)

CHAPTER 12

2000 AND BEYOND

2000
New York Mets (NL) vs. New York Yankees (AL)

New York fans finally got another "Subway Series" in 2000. The last time two teams from the five boroughs had tangled in the postseason was in 1956, although with interleague play, the Mets and Yankees now faced each other during the year. Excitement for an October confrontation began building early in the summer, when Roger Clemens beaned Mike Piazza during one of the midseason matchups and caused him to miss the All-Star Game. Both clubs were highly competitive, with deep pitching, good defense, and experienced players at all the key positions. As they approached the playoffs, however, dreams of a Mets-Yankees World Series began to die. The Yankees lost seven straight to

A new century brought a once-familiar fall theme back to New York—the "subway" series. The powerhouse Yankees met more than token resistance from their crosstown rivals in five tightly played contests.

end the season, and second baseman Chuck Knoblauch was so bad in the field that he could no longer be trusted to throw from second base. The Mets struggled to play .500 ball in September and watched the Braves take the division title once again.

During the postseason, however, both teams came alive. The Yankees survived tough series with the Mariners and the young Oakland A's to win their third consecutive pennant. The Mets, led by unknown rookie Timo Perez and 40-year-old John Franco, squeezed past the Giants and then defeated the Cardinals, who had done them the favor of beating the Braves. While the rest of the country greeted the Subway Series with a yawn, the mood in New York reached a fever pitch. The pumped-up Mets were given a slight edge against the aging Yankees, who were battered and bruised—but still very, very dangerous.

Game One found veteran backup Jose Vizcaino at second base for the Yankees, despite the fact that Luis Sojo had played well in the playoffs. Vizcaino rewarded Joe Torre's confidence with four hits, the last of which drove in the winning run in the bottom of the 12th inning. The 4-3 nail-biter took a record 4 hours, 51 minutes, to play, and it might have ended sooner had the Mets played a little heads-up baseball. Todd Zeile and Jay Payton failed to run out slow rollers that started foul and ended up fair. Perez ran half-speed on a Zeile double (assuming the ball was a home run) and was nailed at the plate on a nice relay from Derek Jeter. The Yankees scored six runs the next night, while Clemens held the Mets scoreless through eight innings. His fine performance was marred by a bizarre incident in the first inning, when he faced Piazza for the first time since hitting him in the head. Piazza

fouled off a pitch, and the head of his shattered bat rolled out to the mound. Clemens picked it up and heaved it in Piazza's direction—an act Clemens could not explain and for which he was later fined. The never-say-die Mets nearly tied the game in the ninth off Jeff Nelson and Mariano Rivera but came up a run short, 6-5.

The excitement continued in Game Three as the Mets treated their fans at Shea Stadium to a great win. They overcame a 12-strikeout performance by Orlando Hernandez to win 4-2 on key hits by Zeile and outfielder Benny Agbayani. The Game Four enthusiasm at Shea was dampened after just one pitch, when Jeter belted a Bobby Jones fastball over the leftfield fence. The Yankees

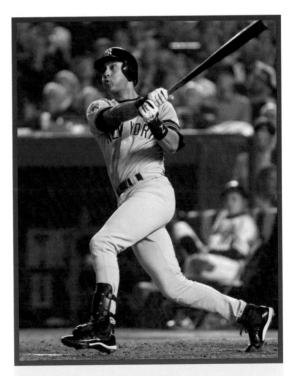

Derek Jeter follows through on his solo home run, hit off Mets starting pitcher Al Leiter, during sixth-inning action in Game Five of the 2000 World Series.

scored single runs in the second and third to take a 3-0 lead, then handed the game to the bullpen, which sealed a 3-2 victory. The Mets hung tough in Game Five, which went into the ninth tied 2-2. Al Leiter, pitching the game of his life, began to tire after striking out Tino Martinez and Paul O'Neill to start the inning. A full-count walk to Jorge Posada and a single to Scott Brosius brought Sojo to the plate. He went with an outside pitch and grounded a seeing-eye hit to right-field. Payton scooped the ball up and threw it home, where it arrived at the same time Posada did. The ball hit Posada and bounced away, enabling Brosius to score. Rivera got the final three outs to wrap up the series.

Yankees 4
  Best Players: Derek Jeter
                (.864 SA, 6 R);
                Paul O'Neill (.474 BA)
Mets 1
  Best Player: John Franco
                (1 W, 0.00 ERA)

2001
Arizona Diamondbacks (NL) vs. New York Yankees (AL)

When the postseason began, few believed the Yankees would be returning to the World Series for a fourth straight year. The Seattle Mariners, winners of 116 games, looked unbeatable. But New York, inspired by the rescue work performed in the weeks following the World Trade Center attacks, did the impossible and subdued the Oakland A's in the Division Series and the Mariners in the ALCS. The Yankees won behind the pitching of Roger Clemens, Andy Pettitte, and new-comer Mike Mussina, who went a combined 52-24 during the year. The New York offense sputtered all season, giving fans in the Bronx grave concerns.

The Diamondbacks were the brainchild of owner Jerry Colangelo, who also owned basketball's Phoenix Suns. Colangelo had tried without success to assemble a championship team under the NBA's salary cap. Major League Baseball has no such restriction, so when the Diamondbacks were formed as an expansion team in 1998, Colangelo was like a kid in a candy store. It took only a few seasons for him to put together a pennant winner. Arizona was custom-built for the postseason. It had two talented starting pitchers in Curt Schilling and Randy Johnson; veteran leaders in Mark Grace, Matt Williams, Luis Gonzalez, and Steve Finley; seasoned role players in Craig Counsell, Danny Bautista, Damian Miller, and Reggie Sanders; and a confident manager in ex-broadcaster Bob Brenly. The team's only weakness was its injury-riddled bullpen.

The Diamondbacks won the first two games at home without having to depend on their relievers. Arizona clobbered Mussina in Game One and got a great start out of Schilling, who struck out eight Yankees in a 9-1 victory. In Game Two, Pettitte and Johnson were locked in a pitcher's duel. Williams blasted one of Pettitte's only bad pitches of the night for a three-run homer to win the game 4-0. The Yankees took Game Three in New York, 2-1, behind the stellar hurling of Clemens and Mariano Rivera.

A good World Series became a great one in Game Four, when 22-year-old Byung-Hyun Kim relieved Schilling with a 3-1 lead in the bottom of the eighth. The Korean submarine-ball specialist befuddled the Yankees, striking out four of the first five

BEST SPIRIT IN TOUGH TIMES: 2001 WORLD SERIES

The 2001 World Series was the first major sports championship played after the September 11 terrorist attacks. Because the regular season was postponed for a week, the series went into the month of November for the first time. Luckily, the weather cooperated, as New York experienced an unusually mild autumn.

The Yankees, who had beaten two younger, better teams in the playoffs to reach the World Series, gave their city a much-needed lift with three straight nail-biting victories at Yankee Stadium. The Diamondbacks, a club built around gritty veterans, tried to ignore the mystique of the Bronx Bombers.

In years past, most people had rooted against the Yankees in the World Series. George Steinbrenner's pinstriped stars represented big-city arrogance, and they always had the money to go out and purchase an "extra player" whenever they needed one. It was hard to root against the battle-scarred New Yorkers this time, however. A lot of fans simply hoped for an entertaining World Series—something to take their minds off the September 11 tragedy and its aftermath.

These two teams did that and more. With a combination of late-inning heroics, big contributions from the little guys, and fantastic performances by the superstars, they delivered a World Series for the ages.

batters he faced. With two out in the ninth, Tino Martinez—who had been hitless in the series—socked a two-run homer to tie the score. Derek Jeter won the game an inning later with a homer to rightfield. Game Five saw the Yankees stage another ninth-inning comeback, when Scott Brosius hit a two-run blast off Kim to knot the score at 2-2. Alfonso Soriano drove in the winning run for New York in the 12th inning.

The Diamondbacks evened things at 3-3 with a 15-2 victory after the series moved back to Arizona. This set up a dramatic seventh game, which went into the bottom of the ninth with the Yankees ahead 2-1. With Rivera on the mound, New York seemed assured of a fourth straight world championship. But the Diamondbacks showed that they could stage a gritty comeback, too. Two hits sandwiched around a throwing error tied the score. After a hit batter, Gonzalez came to the plate with the bases loaded. The man who had launched a career-best 57 homers during the regular season won the World Series with a blooper over New York's drawn-in infield.

Diamondbacks 4
  Best Players: Curt Schilling
                (3 starts, 1.69 ERA);
                Randy Johnson, (3 W)
Yankees 3
  Best Player: Roger Clemens
                (19 K, 1.35 ERA)

For More Information

Some Good Books on the World Series

The 20th Century Baseball Chronicle. Lincolnwood, IL: Publications International, 1992.

Cockcroft, James D. *Latinos in Béisbol.* Danbury, CT: Franklin Watts, 1996.

Gilbert, Thomas. *Baseball and the Color Line.* Danbury, CT: Franklin Watts, 1995.

Lansche, Jerry. *Glory Fades Away.* Dallas, Texas: Taylor Publishing, 1991.

Neft, David, and Richard Cohen. *The World Series.* New York: St. Martin's Press.

Neft, David, Richard Cohen, and Michael Neft. *The Sports Encyclopedia: Baseball.* New York: St. Martin's Press.

Nemec, David. *The Great Encyclopedia of 19th Century Major League Baseball.* New York: Donald I. Fine Books, 1997.

Reichler, Joseph, ed. *The World Series.* New York: Simon and Schuster.

Schoor, Gene. *The History of the World Series.* New York: William Morrow & Co., 1990.

Seymour, Harold. *Baseball: The Golden Age.* New York: Oxford University Press, 1971.

The Sporting News Official World Series Records. *St. Louis, Missouri: The Sporting News.*

Total Baseball. New York: Total Sports.

Index

Page numbers in *italics* indicate illustrations.

About the Author

Mark Stewart ranks among the busiest sportswriters today. He has produced hundreds of profiles on athletes past and present and has authored more than 80 books, including all 10 titles in **The Watts History of Sports.** A graduate of Duke University, Stewart is currently president of Team Stewart, Inc., a sports information and resource company in New Jersey.